Cecily Pouchet Alexander
IMMIGRATION, RACE AND SURVIVAL

From Trinidad to Canada: Living in Parallel Worlds

Immigration, Race and Survival
Copyright © 2021 by Cecily Pouchet Alexander

All rights reserved. No part of this publication may be reproduced, distributed, or transmitted in any form or by any means, including photocopying, recording, or other electronic or mechanical methods, without the prior written permission of the author, except in the case of brief quotations embodied in critical reviews and certain other non-commercial uses permitted by copyright law.

This work is a memoir: a true story of the author's life, as she remembers it. Some names of people, places, and businesses have been changed to protect individual privacy.

Tellwell Talent
www.tellwell.ca

ISBN
978-0-2288-5676-4 (Paperback)

Dedication

I dedicate this book to my mother, Elsie Pouchet, who, by her example and love, made me who I am today

Table of Contents

Dedication iii
Foreword
by Andrew Camman L.L.B. vii

Introduction xi
Chapter 1   Diego Martin, Trinidad: Early Years 1
Chapter 2   Port of Spain: 6 – 10 years old 18
Chapter 3   Diego Martin: 11-18 years old 32
Chapter 4   Immigration to Canada: Edmonton,
            Alberta, 1969-70 43
Chapter 5   Toronto, Ontario, 1970 - 1972 55
Chapter 6   Guelph, Ontario, 1972 – 1976 67
Chapter 7   Montreal, Quebec, 1976 to 1977 &
            Toronto, Ontario, 1977-1978 84
Chapter 8   Madison, Ontario, 1978-1979: Hopewell
            Hospital First Job, Marriage 94
Chapter 9   Franklin, Ontario, 1979-1986: Restora
            Care, Children 97
Chapter 10 Greenville, Ontario, 1986-1995: Ultra Care
            Hospital 108
Chapter 11 Professional and Personal Development
            Employment, Equity, Diversity and Race 131
Chapter 12 Guelph, Ontario, 1995 – 1998: MBA, Job
            Hunting, Teaching 142

Chapter 13	Ashford, Ontario, 1998 – 2011: Cornerstone Hospital 156
Chapter 14	Retirement from Hospital & Clinical Dietetics, 2011 – Present 200

Conclusion 215
Appendix A A History of Race Relations in Trinidad 224
Appendix B Examples of Microaggressions 236
Appendix C Glossary 238
Acknowledgements 243
Bibliography 245
About the Author 251

Foreword
by Andrew Camman L.L.B.

If you think you have climbed and conquered the racist mountain and now declare, "I'm not a racist," then reading this book will show you the mountain range beyond. While this book dashes our self-delusions about racism it does so with a message of hope.

I am a racist. I believe that we all are. What perhaps distinguishes liberal racism from KKK racism is that we accept that it's wrong and we fight it. However, like the alcoholic step program, we must begin with the admission: "Hi, my name is liberal Canadian and I am a racist." Cecily's story of survival shows the immutable truth of this. It also shows that while our generation may always be "recovering" there is hope for recovery as long as we are willing to accept the truth, and as long as there are people like Cecily around to tell it.

I am the lawyer referred to in Cecily's book. I have known and loved Cecily and Wayne for many decades. As her lawyer, and more importantly as her friend, I have gone through many of the traumas she describes in her book. No, let me correct that liberal fantasy; I was with her during those traumas but I did not "go through them" any more than one could go through another's cancer by holding their hand.

I was there when a store owner insisted her son swore at him when he stuttered so badly it was apparent that the storeowner had misidentified the only colored child in the group. I was there when Cecily went over borders and was questioned while I went straight through. I was obviously present when Cecily struggled with mistreatment by her managers in two local hospitals. I was there, but I never went through it with her. I was just there. I was just there until this book put me in it with her. Her simple, frank writing style made me feel her pain and realize the incredible strength that victims of racism must have to survive.

To me Cecily has always been a woman of color. I don't see her as white and never did. She wouldn't have let me. She has always been and always will be my Caribbean Queen (my pet name for her). We may have to add "the unconquerable." When you read her story, you will appreciate that she has earned this moniker. I have sat through post-Trinidad trips with her and Wayne. Cecily would detail how she had carefully planned each matching set of outfits for each event while Wayne's greatest concern was where he had the best rum. Perhaps this is a metaphor for Cecily, who is as important for what we can't see as for what we can. Perhaps it parallels her struggle; while some of us saw her clothes, others could not stop staring at her flattish - but beautiful - nose. There is poignancy and an Ann Frank diary quality to this book. Cecily shows us what lies beneath her skin color in an innocent, vulnerable way. As a white, human rights lawyer, I have prided myself on the ability to empathize with the victims of racism and prejudice. Cecily's story has taught me how wrong I was to celebrate my anti-racist accomplishments. I have known her all these years and assumed that her racism experience wasn't like deep-south racism, so it did not occur to me she was a victim, even as I witnessed her victimization. That I attribute to her resilience and ability to carry on as if her armour had protected her from prejudice. And to some extent it had. Liberals must learn that victims who refuse to be seen as victims still are. The greatest lesson may be that victims must survive, not as victims, but as conquerors. Cecily has suffered, I recognize that now, but the book you are about to read stands as testament to Cecily the Conquering Caribbean Queen.

I am sorry that Cecily suffered through our Canadian racism, but I am thankful her book took me, and those like me, up one more step to recovery.

Introduction

My name is Cecily (Pouchet) Alexander. I was born in Trinidad in the West Indies in 1950 and immigrated to Canada in 1969 at the age of nineteen. I grew up in a middle-class family in Trinidad. I am of mixed race/colored: African, French, Spanish, Scottish and British. My family was very proud of who they were; they were educated and accomplished, and this pride was instilled in me from an early age. My maternal grandfather was a pharmacist, my great-uncle was a magistrate and received a commendation from England at his retirement, my paternal grandfather was in charge of communications at Fort George in Tobago at the beginning of the twentieth century, and my father and his three brothers held high positions in the civil service.

Like many middle-class Trinidadians, I had a charmed life and was indulged by my extended family. Race and class were important to my family. Race has many definitions and meanings. My meaning is sociological. It refers to physical differences that groups and cultures consider socially significant. In Trinidad the physical differences that were valued were Caucasian: straight noses, finer lips, straight hair and white skin. Lighter brown was preferred to darker brown skin. Class and social standing were also highly valued, even more than skin color by some.

In Trinidad, whites have always been in the minority, with Blacks, mixed race/coloreds and East Indians in the majority. My childhood and youth in Trinidad did not prepare me for Canadian racism. Although I grew up in a classist and racialized society in post-colonial Trinidad, I didn't directly experience racism before I came to Canada. Given my upbringing and naiveté, I came to Canada with the expectation of equal treatment, and instead, experienced prejudice for not being white.

My first experiences of racism in Canada were shortly after my arrival. These experiences led me to explore who I am in Canada as a mixed race/colored person and how Canadians have seen me. My "asserted identity" - educated and middle class - was significantly different from Canadians "assigned identity" - Black and therefore poor and disadvantaged. Very early I understood that being colored or of mixed race had no meaning in Canada; in Canada I was Black, and being Black included many of the stereotypes that are associated with Blackness. I use mixed race in my memoir because it is still a descriptive category in the Trinidad and Tobago census and is useful in differentiating race in Trinidad from racial descriptions in other cultures.

I don't think racism in Canada is a lot different from racism in the United States, although Canadians like to think that they are different. This similarity, and Canadian's perception of difference is mainly because Canadians' understanding of racism is based on their knowledge of Blacks and slavery in the United States, rather than a knowledge of the history of slavery in Canada. In colonial Canada slavery did exist, for about 200 years, although the numbers of slaves were fewer. Certainly, the treatment of free Loyalist Blacks and their descendants in Nova Scotia would today be considered racist.

But this is not something that has been taught in Canadian history books. Canadians' knowledge of slavery in Canada tends to be limited to the fact that Canada was a destination on the Underground Railroad for American Blacks escaping slavery in the U.S. And of course, this says nothing about the racist treatment of Canada's indigenous peoples.

Another theme in this memoir is that the United States and Trinidad have different histories of slavery, and that this contributed to my naiveté about race when I immigrated to Canada. One major difference between the United States and the Caribbean and Trinidad in particular, is that the population and governance of Trinidad is Black. In Trinidad, East Indians, Blacks and mixed race are the majority, while Blacks in the United States are in the minority. Slavery was abolished in Trinidad a quarter century before the United States. Trinidad didn't have segregated schools, eating places, churches, bathrooms, transportation, or accommodation. Jim Crow laws and the Klu Klux Klan were U.S. phenomena.

My memoir takes the reader through my exploration and understanding of prejudice and racism. My most significant experiences of racism have been in work environments and have been perpetrated mostly by other women. As a feminist this makes me doubly sad. I now have a newer language that helps me understand these experiences: microaggressions, covert snubs and insults that are negative and target marginalized groups; microinvalidations, which exclude the reality of a person of color; and critical race theory, the view that the law and legal institutions are inherently racist and that race itself, instead of being biologically grounded and natural, is a socially constructed concept that is used by white people to further their economic and political interests at the expense of people of color.

These are terms that are now commonly used to describe racism, but they weren't part of my vocabulary when I was experiencing racism. I knew that what I was experiencing was wrong and more importantly, that these "wrongs" were being done to me because I was Black; they were not being done to anyone white in the organizations in which I experienced them.

Canada is a majority white country so it is not surprising that most of my friends are white. The two major relationships that I describe in my memoir are with white men. Choices of friends and mates is based (for me) on similarities in ideas, people I enjoy being with, who I can do similar things with, and who are like-minded. I have West Indian and Black friends also who fit my definition of compatibility, but this doesn't mean that because someone is Black that we are instantly compatible. One concern I do have is the lack of acceptance and the consciousness of many Canadians. Racism does exist in Canada. Discussions of racism with my white friends sometimes results in "white fragility" where they become defensive and wounded, even angry, in response. Discussions of race do not come up very often with my white friends and when they do, many say they don't see race and my color. I hope reading my memoir will enlighten some on the pervasive existence of racism, and by doing this motivate them to make individual changes in how they see and react to Black people; to see that it is not enough to be "not racist," one must be anti-racist. Collectively, this might result in some change occurring. I am not so idealistic as to think that this will happen any time soon.

Throughout history, the subjugation of Blacks has had an economic advantage, and in Canada, as in most capitalist societies, most people will not be economically disadvantaged in order to effect social change.

Chapter 1

Diego Martin, Trinidad: Early Years

I was born in 1950 in Trinidad and Tobago, while it was still, nominally at least, a British colony. My earliest memories are from when I was just 3 years old. We lived in a big white house at the top of a hill, on Crystal Stream Avenue, in what is now a suburb of Port of Spain called Diego Martin. Our house was nestled in, away from the avenue. The corner lot had a big breadfruit tree and a large hedge of beautiful crotons. On the other side of our house were three empty lots lined with coconut trees.

I spent most of my time with my nanny, Mary. From this tender age I felt a deep love for my mother. She was beautiful and smart, not like other mothers who walked around in house dresses. She worked in the city, dressed up every morning and went to work.

My mother, Elsie Pouchet

My memories of my father are vaguer at this age. I know he came home every day for lunch. Mary, our maid, would set the table for two places, one for my father and one for me. He would arrive and say, "How's my little girl today?" He would ask the usual questions about school and he would tease me saying something like, "How is your boyfriend, "big-head" Darrel?" At the time, Darrel was my friend from across the street. He was my age and I played with him most days.

My brother, Edward, was five years older than me and during the week he went to school in Port of Spain and often stayed at my grandmother's house or at my great uncle's house one street over. Being in Port of Spain meant he was close to school and all of his friends.

Because I was just three, I only went to school half-days in the mornings. This was a small private school run by Miss Pollards and had about twenty children. I sat on one bench with the three other children who also attended half-days. I was the youngest. At the beginning of September, my three friends went to another bench. They were now in stage two going full-days, so I sat alone in stage one. When Mary came to get me at lunchtime I burst into tears, "All the kids have gone to another bench and I am the only one in stage one."

Mary told me that it was because I only went to school half-days. She said she would take me back in the afternoon if I thought I could handle going to school all day. My big smile was the answer. So, one of the earliest decisions about my education was made by my nanny. Mary would boast and tell this story to anyone who would listen, of the day she made the decision to let me go to school full-time.

I was a happy child. I had lots of toys and I was loved, especially by mummy and nanny. But there was also a possessive love from my aunt Milly. Milly was my mother's sister and was never married, so I became her surrogate daughter. I could get almost anything I wanted because auntie Milly and my mother often competed for my affection.

In the evenings Mary would set the table with mummy's dinner and I would climb on a chair next to her chattering about my day. "Yes I went to school today, yes daddy came home for lunch and I had lunch with him." I wouldn't say much more as talking about daddy always seemed to make her sad. "Guess what mummy? I went to school both in the morning and in the afternoon." "What?" Mummy asked. Thankfully Mary came in to explain that when she went to pick me up at lunch time I was sad and crying because the other three children on my bench had moved to stage two while I was all alone on the stage one bench. Mary told my mother that I was very happy when she took me back in the afternoon because I could move to stage two as well and start going to school both morning and afternoon.

After dinner mummy would often play a few games with me and she would ask me questions about the alphabet and numbers. In our house we had two big bedrooms facing the road; one was my dad's room and the other was my mother's and mine. A smaller third room, facing the back yard, was my brother's room.

Weekends were my favorite time with my family. Every Saturday my father and mother would pile my brother and myself into the car and we would head to Maracas, the main beach along the north coast. At this early age I found the rough waters with large rolling waves exhilarating. This was an outing taken by many families who lived in Port of Spain or in the suburbs like we did. On the drive to Maracas, my brother and I would play our favorite game, spotting the mileposts.

Every quarter mile, the original road-builders had erected a concrete mile post. Some you could see clearly, but many were hidden by the undergrowth of tropical bushes that grow wildly in those parts. When one appeared we would shout "ONE," and, the person who spotted the most won. My brother always won. I don't think that I won once. I remember we played this game from about the time I was three years old and onwards. At three my brother was eight. Even when I sat in the front seat on my mother's lap I couldn't win. It was only as adults that my brother told me that he had memorized where all the mileposts were and would shout, "One" just a few seconds before it would be visible.

I absolutely loved Maracas. At the beach I was in my element; the blue water, the coconut trees, and the white sand were magical. I would usually build sandcastles with my brother's help or sometimes with help from my mother and father.

The next day, Sunday, always started with church for my mother and Sunday school for my brother and myself. We would head into Port of Spain to the All-Saints Anglican church. All Saints is one of the oldest churches In Trinidad with interesting architecture and spectacular stained-glass windows. More importantly it was the only church my mother's family patronized. My father was Methodist and didn't attend this church. Both my parents loved to entertain and Sunday afternoons were often spent with friends, drinks and delicious food and snacks prepared by my mother. Friends would just drop in. In Trinidad we didn't have formal telephone invitations. Friends would see the gathering and stop in to join the "lime," a Trinidadian word for getting together and hanging out with friends.

At four I became friends with Deanne Harracksingh. She was an East Indian girl who lived across the street. My brother, who was nine already, was friends with her older brother, Michael. Deanne was two years older than me and I would do anything to play dolls with her. She was a bit bossy at six, so I would let her choose which doll she wanted and what make-believe games she wanted to play.

Sometimes Deanne would leave Diego Martin to go to San Fernando to spend time with her extended family there. I would usually be despondent because then I would be stuck playing cricket with the boys in the neighbourhood. My position was "fielding the ball" which usually meant running down the hill to retrieve balls that rolled away from the boys, not actually playing a fielding position. I would be out of breath retrieving these balls for them. Finally, at the end of the game it would be my turn to bat. They would aim to the wicket and always hit it and I would be out by the first ball. You can see why I would pine away for Deanne to return.

With a brother five years older than me, I grew up like an only child; Edward and I didn't often play together. Some of my favourite times were when my mother took me with her to visit with family and friends. My father's two brothers and their families also lived in Diego Martin, just a short car ride from our place. I would get to play catch and other active games with my cousins. It would often be a sad return to our big house with just my parents and me at home.

Although I remember many happy times and times of minor sadness between the ages of three and five years old, there were also times of greater sadness. Most evenings were sad for my mother. I would sit with my mother in our little verandah on the second floor waiting for my dad to get home. My mum would sometimes cry, but if I caught her she would deny it and hug me and tell me how much she loved my brother and me and how we were her life. I would promise to never leave her, and that I would always be there for her. I realized even then that this sadness had to do with my father's absence. My mother and father did not really argue or fight a lot. They would discuss things - about the house, the maids, my brother, myself – but that was not what made her sad.

One day when I was five, things came to a head. My brother, who was ten, was shining my father's shoes for Lodge. My father was a Mason at Lodge. To me Lodge was this secret society that men went to. I learned later that the Masons were made up of businessmen, judges, lawyers, police officers of high rank, customs officers; people of influence were sought out to join the society. The mission of the Masons was mainly to establish collective influence over their self-interest from a business perspective. In my childhood in Trinidad I thought its main focus was to make better men out of good men, which, in the context of this story, is very ironic.

For some reason my father wasn't pleased with the shoe shine job my brother was doing and my father began to shout at my brother. My mother jumped in to object. He shoved her and pushed her out of the way. She fell backwards. My mother was shocked.

She said, "I have put up with your philandering, but shoving me down in my own house is the first and also the last time I will be so disrespected." She ordered my father to leave the house, and went to her room. My father left us that evening. Even at that tender age I understood, from listening to the conversations of my aunts, that my father had another woman. This was why my mother was so sad. His rough treatment of my brother and pushing her down had been the last straw.

It has taken me until adulthood to analyze what must have gone wrong in my parent's marriage. They had been sweethearts for a long time before they got married. It seems to be the belief of many Trinidadian men, however, that they have a right to have affairs. This sense of entitlement can be seen in many other parts of the world where men have affairs, but I find it still pervasive today in Trinidad. Apparently both my grandfathers had illegitimate children, and I have heard of many friends' fathers who have done the same thing.

I am still saddened today when I reflect on my mother's physical and emotional health at that time. She had two miscarriages before my brother Edward was born. She had another miscarriage before my birth. All three of her miscarriages were second trimester, so she knew the gender: all male; my father was inconsolable. I realize now that by the age of 43, my mother had become a brittle diabetic. Although treatment for certain forms of diabetes had been known since the discovery of insulin in Canada in the 1920's, in Trinidad it was a disease that was largely untreated. So my mother spent most of her years suffering from this disease and it got out of control.

She described having to be on bed rest for a couple months before having me. A midwife-nurse named Miss Thomas looked after her often during this period. My mother credited Nurse Thomas with saving my life. Another event that my mother described to me was my father's reaction to having a daughter. He came to see her just after my birth and when he found out that I was a girl, he "steuped" (sucked air in through his teeth; a Trinidadian body language response that shows annoyance or disapproval) and walked out.

Tired, overworked, an uncontrolled diabetic and emotionally saddened by her husband's infidelity, I cannot think of my mother as being capable of being responsive to my father's advances. My father, as many men did in the 1950's, found a mistress.

My brother has said to me that he thought the affair our father had at that time was almost certainly not his first. My father was good looking and popular; he was a well-known cricketer on the West Indian cricket team. He would have been considered a "catch" for sure. When I thought about it, I agreed with my brother, and I'm sure my mother also knew. She put up with it until the abusive incident with my brother tipped the balance and she kicked my father out.

It may sound surprising that in 1955 a woman could order her husband to leave the family home. This was a time when women were often trapped in unhappy marriages. Men were typically the sole income earners and owners of the family home. Divorce was not common, unlike today. I certainly did not have any friends growing up with divorced parents. To understand our family situation back then, you need to understand a little more about my mother. My mother was an early entrepreneur. She had convinced my grandmother to part with her inheritance while she was still alive. My mother then proceeded to buy what would become prime real estate in Diego Martin. She sold half of the land to another family, the Turpins, and was able to build our family home from the proceeds of the sale. My father owned nothing; the house, the land, and the other 3 adjacent lots of land all belonged to my mother. So when my mother told him to leave, he had to move out.

To this day, I still haven't met anyone as strong as my mother. I looked up to her. She had an excellent job working as an assistant to the chief operating officer at the Anglo American Caribbean Commission. She probably made more money than my father, which was unusual in the 1950's. My father had a government job as a price control officer. His assessments of small business owners could send someone to court to be charged with excessive pricing of goods and the owners would have to pay large fines.

His job was important in its own right but did not pay well.

My father was famous in Trinidad, not for his government job, but for his cricket career. Trinidadians lived and breathed cricket, and my father was a very good player, a left hand spin bowler, on the Trinidad cricket team in the 1930's and 1940's. On match days you would see men on the street walking around with their transistor radios at their ears listening to matches. I was named after my father Cecil Pouchet. As I grew up, people would see my name, Cecily Pouchet, and immediately connect me with my famous father. Note at this time the cricket team was all white except for my father.

Cecil Pouchet, 2nd from left, seated

My father and mother dated for at least six years before they were married. He was the oldest of four boys and one sister. The Pouchet name, was important to him. He would say to me from a young age, "Remember you are a Pouchet." I never knew my grandfather, but his picture was of a Frenchman, probably of mixed race. He represented himself as a white Trinidadian to his family, but he was probably colored. The term "colored" or "mixed" is seen as a distinct group in Trinidad and is still represented in our census as a distinct group. The family history as it was related to me described my great-grandfather as coming to Trinidad from the French island of Martinique. Many people, white French plantation owners and colored French creoles, had immigrated to Trinidad from French West Indian colonies all throughout the 19th century, ever since the French revolution had made remaining in those French colonies less hospitable for "royalist" families. One such French immigrant with the family name Pouchet is mentioned in de Verteuil's book: Trinidad's French Legacy. This may be one of my earlier ancestors.

Grandfather, Lewis Pouchet

My father's family was relatively successful in Trinidad, including my father's three brothers. One brother, my uncle Errol, was the deputy permanent secretary in the Ministry of Health. Another brother, my uncle Lionel, was an air traffic controller at the International Airport. My father's youngest brother, my uncle

Dick, was a land surveyor who had trained both in Trinidad and the UK. My grandfather, Lewis Pouchet, born sometime between 1885-1890, and my grandmother Ethel McEachrane, raised their family in Tobago. They had a grand house on the road up to Fort George, an English fort built in the early 19th century, and Lewis Pouchet worked there in communications. Fort George is a famous landmark that is now visited by tourists in Tobago. It has beautiful grounds and a spectacular view of the harbour. My grandfather died at the early age of fifty in the 1930's. Before he passed away, however, he moved the family to Trinidad, to a house on Fitt Street in Woodbrook, so that his four sons could attend school in Trinidad. They all went to Queen's Royal College, one of the premier secondary schools in Trinidad.

My mother was the youngest of three girls. My mother's father, my grandfather, was a druggist with his own dispensary. He managed an estate in Blanchicheuse on the north coast of Trinidad. His dispensary was called the "Electric Pharmacy", it being one of the only dispensaries with electricity in 1905. He went through the countryside on horseback meeting country folk who needed care. His name was Henry Aumaitre. Like the Pouchet name, Henry Aumaitre's predecessors would have been at least partly French as illustrated by his French last name. He was well-educated for that time. Born in 1874, he died in 1908 from pneumonia. Penicillin hadn't been discovered yet.

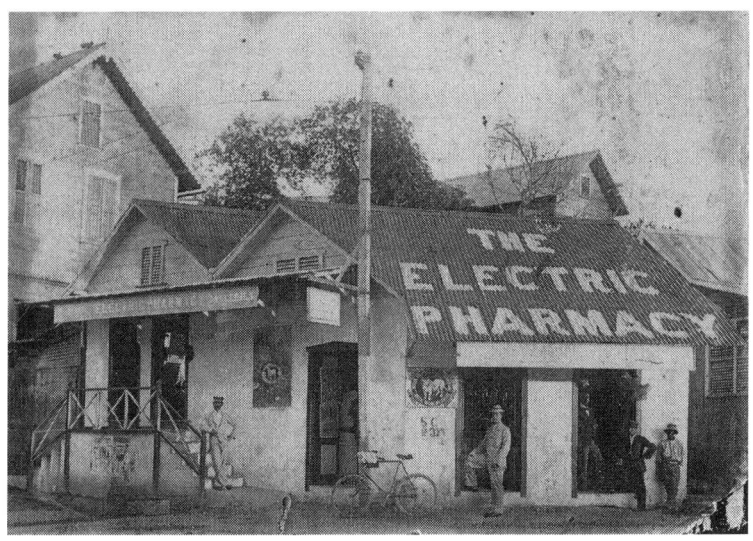

The Electric Pharmacy. My grandfather standing at the front door

He left enough land and money for my grandmother's brother, my great-uncle Walter Harris, to move his sister Georgiana and her three girls, my mother and her two sisters, to Port of Spain. He lived in Woodford Street with his mother and sister, great-aunt Violet (Tantie Vie). He bought a house on the next street, Picton Street, for his sister and nieces to live in. He was also able to purchase another house in Woodbrook for his sister to rent and use the money to maintain her family. Women of class still didn't work at the turn of the century. Also, my mother and her sisters were very young, six, four and one, so my grandmother stayed at home to look after them.

My maternal grandfather, Henry Aumaitre

I was proud of my great-uncle Walter. He was respected in our community and many came to him to help solve their problems. In later years, Walter was awarded the Imperial Service Order medal for his distinguished career.

Uncle Walter Hampton Harris's "Imperial Service Order" medal. This medal was established under the statutes of the Imperial Service Order, by King Edward VII

Great-uncle Walter also generously supplemented his extended family's income. He had a job as a well-known and respected Magistrate in Port of Spain. It was because my mother came from this middle-class and successful family that she was later able to own our home in Crystal Stream, Diego Martin. When my grandmother sold her rental house in Woodbrook, my mother convinced my grandmother to give her inheritance to her early. It was with this that she bought the land in Diego Martin. There were enough lots to build ten houses, and my mother was a shrewd businesswoman.

We continued to live at our home in Crystal Stream for one more year after my father left. I was six years old. It was a great place to live; there were lots of open spaces and a river at the end of our property. Crystal Stream and Diego Martin at that time consisted of many East Indian families, colored creoles, Blacks and a few white families. The friends I played with, in addition to my two sets of cousins, were the girls in three Indian families that surrounded our house. My best friend was Deanne Harracksingh from an East Indian family across the street.

One of the places I loved to visit was my Uncle Dan's estate in Diego Martin. He was my godfather and had every imaginable fruit tree on his estate. You could wander through the endless growth of sweet cherry, plum, star apple, mango, tangerine and orange trees. His main helper was a tall, Black, jack-of-all-trades man called "Sleepy" because his eyes were always half closed. Whenever we visited, Sleepy would put me on his shoulders and take me to pick whatever fruits I wanted. I was always excited to visit.

Occasionally my mother would use Sleepy to do some minor repairs around our house. It was on one of these occasions that I was violated and molested by Sleepy. He took me under my mother's big four-poster bed and exposed himself to me and put my little, five-year old hands on his penis. Like all molesters, he made me promise not to tell. Thank goodness he didn't say that he would hurt me if I told on him, so I did, about a week later, in a conversation with my mother. She was shocked, upset, and angry. She went over to Uncle Dan's and Auntie Lorna's home and Sleepy was fired. In present days, of course, this is an offense for which Sleepy would have been arrested and put in jail.

What do you tell a five year old? My mother' explanation was all about "private parts" and that Sleepy had done a "bad" thing and that I shouldn't let anyone other than my aunts and my mother touch my privates. It was all very confusing, but I do not remember being scared. In a way, I was sorry that Sleepy lost his job and I wouldn't ever see him again. Why couldn't they make him promise never to do it again as they had said to me?

My great-uncle Walter died when I was six, leaving my great-aunt, Tantie Vie, to live and manage their big house alone. This house had four big bedrooms. It was an old fashion structure where the kitchen was a separate building away from the house. The yard was huge with a big Julie mango tree and many sheds. One shed was empty and that was where I played with my friends in our own fort. Tantie Vie asked my mother to come to Port of Spain to live with her.

Moving to the city was great for my brother, Edward; he would be closer to his friends and his public school. Edward attended All Saints E.C., which was situated on Tragarite Road at the bottom of Picton Street where my grandmother and aunts lived. The move to Port of Spain would also allow me to attend a private school with my cousins in Port of Spain. I would also be able to see my dad more frequently as he worked in Port of Spain at that time.

Chapter 2

Port of Spain: 6 - 10 years old

My years in Port of Spain were happy years. I had lots of freedom to ride my bike through the streets of New Town and Woodbrook. Beyond that there was a boundary that I couldn't go past by myself or with my friends. But we knew every mango, plum and cherry tree in the city and one of our favorite things to do was raid the fruit trees. We would then head to one of our homes to make chow. This was mixture of fruit with lots of salt and hot peppers. Unlike Canada, in Trinidad we mix many of our fruits with salt and pepper.

In Port of Spain, I was surrounded by my family. I lived with great-aunt, Tantie Vie. I used to say then and still do now, that she was more Victorian than Queen Victoria. She demonstrated good manners, always spoke proper English, and she thought it was her duty to teach this to me. If I got upset, I would put my hands on my hips and "talk back." She had the power to make me cry with words only. When I did talk back, she would say, "Are you from behind the bridge?", or, "Are you a washer woman?", or the worst, "That behaviour is common and vulgar." I would burst into tears.

Tantie Vie was very religious and her volunteer work included doing all the ironing of the fine linens for the vestry at All Saints Anglican Church at the Savannah. The maids couldn't touch these holy items. Tantie Vie ironed them herself. She loved to invite Father Howe, our English minister, to tea. Her maid would prepare a high English tea. Tea consisted of fresh scones, cream and jam, cucumber, egg and ham sandwiches with the crusts removed, accompanied by sponge cake. The highlight of his visits would be a performance by me where I would memorize and recite long poems, chosen, of course, by Tantie Vie. I was proud of my ability to perform "choral speaking" which involves passages that are read aloud and enunciated clearly.

Just one street over, on Picton Street, was where my grandmother lived with my two aunts, auntie Ann (Andrea) and auntie Milly (Mildred). My grandmother was the disciplinarian. I had a six o'clock curfew. At six o'clock, just as the sun fell below the horizon, Trinidad would go from dusk to dark in a matter of minutes. The Catholic Church, Saint Patrick's, three houses away from my grandmother's and aunts' homes, had a big church bell that they rang every day at six p.m.

When I heard the bell ring, my job was to get on my bike and head home, riding like crazy. Usually I could be home no later than five or ten minutes past six, especially if I was playing with my friends in the nearby park. The problem was, I began to prefer playing in the park by the fire station on Roberts Street - over ten minutes away! If I was at that park, I would almost always be too late. My grandmother would strap me with her grey belt. At the age of seven, I knew that this was unfair.

Even at that early age I knew how to negotiate with my mother and I knew that she wouldn't like the fact that I was being strapped. My mother shared her feelings with me from a young age and me with her. One night I said to her that I found it unfair that so many people could spank or punish me. I said I thought that she should be the only one allowed to do this. My mother agreed. The family would have to tell her if I misbehaved and when she got home from work she would decide on my punishment.

That was pretty much the end of my corporal punishment days. I received no more spankings from my grandmother on

Picton Street. But I lived at Woodford with my Tantie Vie. She was not pleased with my mother's decision and was determined to show me who was smarter. Over the holidays, July and August vacations, Tantie Vie was in charge. If I misbehaved at two in the afternoon, she would make me sit in her great chair for hours waiting for my mother to come home to decide on my punishment. By that time, I would be begging to get a spanking over with so I could get back to playing with my friends.

My favorite times with my Tantie Vie were when I could lie with her in bed and she would make up stories. "Once upon a time, there was a little girl," and that little girl was always me. Sometimes I was a princess, other times I was a brave girl who had great adventures. I loved the stories where I grew up in a perfect family with a mum and dad who lived together, like most of my friends' families. Tantie Vie knew all of the family secrets. She told me about her grandfather, my great-great-great-grandfather Harris. He was an Englishman who immigrated to Trinidad from Barbados. He fasted on Sundays and spent the day in a big arm chair, where all he had was a glass of water to drink. She describes him as white, with light-blue eyes. There are no pictures or proof of this, however, so it was probably another made up story.

Port of Spain was different and exciting, and there was a lot to explore. I do remember, however, missing the countryside around Diego Martin. This period marked the beginning of my sense of self awareness. Some days at lunch time I would visit my father at his sister's home. Fathers have a role to play in their daughter's lives, in liking themselves and building their self-esteem. Unfortunately, it was from my father that I learned that my face and features were not "white" enough. He would tell me, "Pull up your nose." I would then spend time holding my nostrils, and holding my breath, in the hopes of making my nose straighter. The other feature was my lips. He would tell me that I should "bite them in." So I would try to decrease the size of my lips by constantly chewing on my bottom lip. Of course none of these techniques worked. My features were mine and they were here to stay.

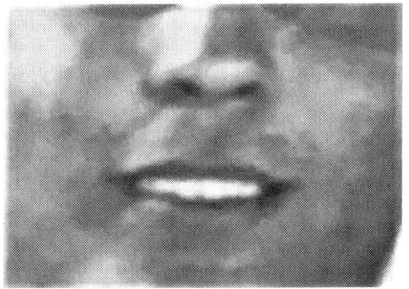

My father's straight nose and thin lips

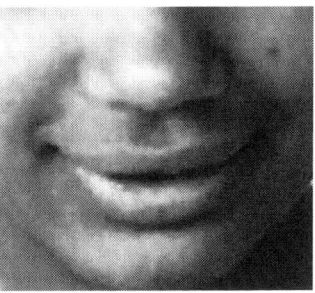

My flat nose and thick lips

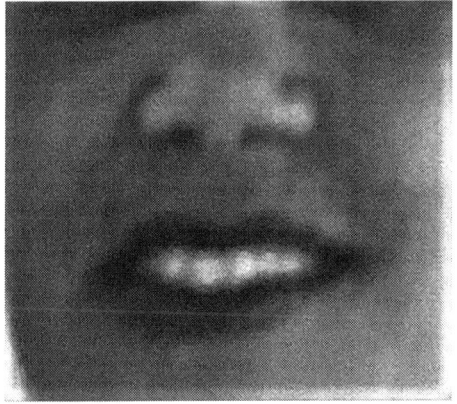

My mother's lips and nose

My mother's nose is wider than mine; I suppose my nose is a cross between my mother's and father's. In looking at these three pictures now, I see that my lips are thicker that both of my parents. There is not much you can do about genes! Unlike my father's undercutting of my appearance, neither my mother nor my aunts ever said anything about my features; I was beautiful in their eyes. I never shared my father's comments with my mother.

My assessment of my hair, however, was all my own, or at least, mirrored the common societal values about Black features. Why didn't I have the same texture hair as my auntie Ann or my mother's "good hair?" At least I could be thankful that my hair was not as kinky as my brother's hair. My aunts would say, "It's a blessing that the girl child has the better hair." Better than my brother's, perhaps, but still not good.

My hair was very thick. I had a full head of hair. I usually wore it in two long braids, or sometimes three; one at the top braided into my other two braids at the back. Saturdays were a big washing hair day. After washing, my mother or my Auntie Milly would lather Brylcreem into my hair and roll it into circles or little buns. When my hair was almost dry they would undo the buns and my hair would be "curled" with ribbons for Sunday school. Monday mornings it would back to braids or plaits again.

The picture above is me at six or seven. This was probably a Sunday because I am dressed up with a handbag and my hair is curled and brushed back with a bow

To this day I am not sure exactly what texture my hair really was because at the tender age of eight my mother took me to the hairdresser to "straighten" my hair. This was done with Jafrees, a strong chemical product that, in addition to straightening your hair, also changed its texture and burned your scalp. It was so strong it would leave scabs on my scalp for a week.

I stopped worrying about my nose when my aunt said, "You have a Hailey Mills nose." Hailey Mills was my hero; if a film star could have a nose like mine, it was good enough for me. Despite my father's comments about my appearance, I liked the way I looked. Of course, as I became a teenager, I developed breasts and a more feminine body and I knew I had a good figure. This was partly because of the feedback I received from males of all ages, and the feedback I received from my female friends. On the whole, I have tended to trust feedback from females more than males because I thought it was more honest. So my overall confidence and self-esteem were quite strong. This is a characteristic that has helped me through many difficult situations, including my future migration to Canada.

It is interesting how you learn about color and race at an early age. I cannot remember any direct conversations about it, but I knew that white or lighter skin was "better." Most of my childhood friends in Port of Spain were Trini whites. The girls, Alana, Cheryl Ann and Pat, and my best male friend at seven, Robert, were all Trini whites, or people who could pass for white. I went to their homes and they came to mine - all except Jacklyn.

Jacklyn was a girlfriend on my street, Woodford Street. She was a Pouchet. Her father, was my father's first cousin. I had a dilemma: what do I call him? In Trinidad we definitely do not use first names for adults, unless they were the "help."

You sometimes called your parents' friends "auntie" or "uncle" or you called them Mister and Mrs. and their last name. I didn't think I could call a cousin of my father Mister Pouchet!

I went with this problem to my father. He looked at me as if I had two heads. "Of course call him Uncle he is your uncle." In spite of my father's answer, I just couldn't because my uncle was married to a Trinidad white. His mother-in-law, Jacklyn's grandmother, lived with them. They made it pretty obvious that they did not like me playing with Jacklyn. Her grandmother even instructed me once to come in through their back door and not the front door. I was defiant and never did this, but I understood at another level what was going on.

This was a secret I couldn't tell either my mother or my father, because if I did, they both would try to fix it their way. Adults tended to deny blatant prejudice and I knew I would be treated worse in the long run. As the saying goes: if looks could kill... I liked playing with Jacklyn, so I didn't address the adults by any names. I continued to be polite, saying, "good morning," or "good afternoon," to whomever answered the door.

The Savannah, the large, central park in Port of Spain, was within walking distance of Woodford Street. Horse races went on frequently at the Savannah and Jacklyn and I went there to bet on the favorites. Yes, at eight years old! We would get the newspaper and write down all the favorites. Not great odds, maybe just two-to-one, but that would double our money, and to us that was great. We would usually come back with more money than we went with. We would go to the Savannah and look for someone in line we thought we could trust and ask him to place our bet. If we won, we also had to find someone who looked honest to pick up our winnings.

One evening, my father came to visit my mother. He had called earlier that day. I overheard my mother saying she would come out to his car to meet him. My great-aunt, Tantie Vie, would not welcome him into our house for what she called "his despicable, disgraceful behaviour." So that evening my father arrived and my mother slipped out with me to greet him. At that time they had been separated for two years.

My father's news was that he wanted to finalize their separation with a divorce. He wanted to marry again. I do not know if my mother had ever expected reconciliation with my father, but this was very difficult for her. She cried and asked him not to do this to her and to my brother and myself. He said that although he was sorry, his mind was made up. My mother fought back with all she had and that was me. She said that I would be forbidden to visit him with his new wife at his new home; he had just built a new house on the St. Augustine Main Road.

They negotiated. At the end of their discussion, they decided that I could continue to see him at his sister's house, my Auntie Angela's place. I could continue to ride my bike to her place to see him as I had already been doing. My brother, however, could visit my father at his new house when he wanted. It would be understandable, perhaps, that I would resent my mother in later years for these decisions. But I understood, even at this early age, how much it would hurt my mother having the person, whom my father had replaced her with, comb my hair, help me get dressed, and read me stories before bed. It would have been too much for her and she would have been too sad when I was gone. One of my strongest desires was to do things that would make my mother happy, to have her laugh again, and not be so sad. So I agreed to her decision. As it turned out, the finality of my father remarrying changed my mother. She began to live again.

I went to Tranquility Girl's Intermediate School for public school. The boys' school was just next to the girls' school separated by a big fence. The boys could not come over to our playground at recess but they did come over after school, mainly to play games with marbles. I was a "tom boy." I could climb any tree and play marbles as well as the boys. I rode my bike not only in New Town or Woodbrook but also all over Port of Spain. My competitive nature, I'm sure, was part of a subconscious need I had to impress my father, who had made it abundantly clear that boys were more important than girls.

I was naturally good at math, but one of my favourite classes was with Frieda McBurney Artman our English teacher. She taught us much more than English literature; she taught us to appreciate nature and she developed our imaginations. She would lead the class onto the grassy part of the school yard and we would all lie on the grass and look up at the sky and let our imagination run wild. I was only eight, and this opened my mind to the power of daydreaming. I could close my eyes and imagine whatever I wanted. In those times I imagined a beautiful world, with both of my parents.

At the corner of the street where Tranquility was located was a hotel with the best plum tree in Port of Spain. I went there frequently with a group of friends to pick its plums. I would be up the tree in minutes and would shake the branches. My friends would collect the plums that fell in a bag and we would share them when we were finished. On one of those days, when I was up in the tree, my mother appeared out of nowhere and demanded I get down and ride my bike home. This time she threatened a severe spanking; I had gone too far. When I got home, instead of coming into the house, I climbed up the mango tree in our yard to the top branch. I said I wasn't coming down and would sleep in the tree that night. By about eight o'clock I had about five adults from the neighbourhood pleading with me to come down. I finally relented. Needless to say my mother had recovered from her initial annoyance and didn't punish me after all. However, I was forbidden to climb the hotel plum tree after that.

It was about this time that my mother decided that I should join the Brownies, the girls' version of the Cub Scouts. I said I had no interest in being a Brownie. From what I had heard from my girlfriends, Brownies spent their time baking, singing and playing silly games. I wanted to be a Scout. I had just visited a big

Scout jamboree – my brother was a Scout. Boys from all over the world were there. He had such a great time! They traded all sorts of things: badges, pins from their countries, and anything you could imagine. I was silent on the drive home. When my mother asked me what was wrong, I said, "Life is so unfair that boys seem to have all the fun." My mother let me brood. She understood, I think, but knew she could do nothing to change it.

It was just weeks later that my mother told me she thought I should take piano lessons. Musically, I had been a disappointment to my mother and my aunts. They all had beautiful voices and sang in the church choir when they were younger. My mother was an embarrassment to me in church: she could sing the high notes clearly, way better than the other parishioners! Meanwhile, I had heard so many times, "This girl child can't carry a tune." So I objected to piano also. The stories from my friends who took piano lessons were that it was worse than Brownies. You sat with a piano teacher for hours and she would strike your knuckles with a ruler if you played the wrong note. I was much too active a child to find piano interesting. To this day, however, I regret that my mother let me have my way. As an adult I would love to be able to read music and be able to play an instrument. It was again about this time that one of my best friends was taking ballet lessons. I went with her to one of her practices and was awestruck. I went home and announced that ballet was what I wanted to do. My mother would not let me get my way. She said, "No. No Brownies, no piano, so no ballet."

My aunty Milly never married and had no children of her own. I loved her dearly and dreamed that when I was older, I would buy her a house of her own to decorate however she wished. You see aunty Milly was also my godmother and very devoted to me. There was actually a competition for my affection between my mother and auntie Milly. I knew this from a very early age. So if I asked my mother for something and she said no, then I would ask auntie Milly next. In the case of ballet lessons, that was exactly what I did. Auntie Milly was only too happy to sign me up and pay for my lessons and she did this for the five years that I took lessons, even adding modern dance to the mix later on.

All of the women in my mother's family were very happy with the changes they saw in me. I was such a tomboy! They thought that I was developing more grace and becoming more of a lady with my dance lessons. I loved ballet. The prize of a year's hard work was a major production at Queen's Hall, in The Performing Arts Theater, in Saint Ann's. I can still remember the production of Arabian Nights where I was part of a group that played the thieves. We danced onto the stage swinging our swords with a bag of stolen treasures over our shoulders and gave a very energetic performance. My family were so pleased by my performance at Queens Hall that they never discussed the devious means I had used to be able to take ballet in the first place.

In Port of Spain, one significant experience I had that I remember today, was with Alvin, the son of our maid, Princess. Another family, the Govia's, lived across the street, and they would sometimes visit us on Saturdays. Alvin, would often accompany his mother to our place on Saturdays and, while she did her work around the house, he would play with me and the Govia kids in the backyard. After lunch one Saturday, my mother told the Govia kids to ask their mother if they could come to Maracas with us. Maracas is the main beach outside Port of Spain. They could and we all piled into my mother's car.

But before the car left the yard, my Tantie Vie came outside in a fluster saying, "Stop the car. Alvin where do you think you are going? Get out of the car now and go to your mother!" Alvin got out and began to cry. I really wanted Alvin to come, but at eight years old I knew better than to protest. It was so unfair; just because he was the maid's child. That memory has stuck with me and at that time I made a pledge to be friends with whomever I wanted. Alvin was just who he was - the maid's son. That may have made all the difference to Tantie Vie, but it wouldn't to me.

Another incident that made a great impression on me was with Sam, who lived on our street. Many streets had what is called a "yard with rooms." These backyard "rooms" were rented out to families; sometimes a whole family and their kids could be living in just one room. One sunny day I saw Sam with his little daughter Suzie. Suzie was two or three years old. She had a T-Shirt that was too small for her and no panties. That wasn't unusual; many kids under ten ran around naked, although it was less common in the city.

Sam had Suzie standing on the neighbour's fence and he was spreading the lips of her vagina and looking at it. I froze. I knew this was wrong. I remembered the incident with Sleepy. No one should touch your privates and that was what Sam was doing to Suzie. Should I tell someone? I was told only my aunts and my mother could undress me or see my privates. This was Susie's dad, I knew he was doing a bad thing, but I didn't tell.

My grandmother died when I was ten years old. As we were from a close extended family, I remember the day leading up to her death very clearly. After the doctor left he told us that her heart was failing and she didn't have long to live. We all took turns in saying goodbye, even me. She told me she loved me, and I had to be a good girl and obey my mother and family and then she gave me her prized gold bracelets as the youngest girl child in the family. I treasure them to this day. Her funeral was different from Canada in that the coffin was in our parlour at home and after the church service the immediate family walked behind the coffin to Lapeyrouse cemetery. At the graveside when the grave diggers began to lower the coffin I asked if I could see Grandma one more time. They lifted the coffin back up and lay it down and opened it. I looked at her peaceful face and was inconsolable.

Shortly after my grandmother's funeral, my Tantie Vie decided to sell her home on Woodford Street and move to Picton Street with my aunts. They built a self-contained apartment for her. The property was narrow at the front but had a long yard so there was lots of room for Tantie Vie, but it meant that my mother, my brother, and I returned to our home in Crystal Stream in Diego Martin. I was elated. My best girlfriend between the ages of four and six had been Deanne. She was from an East Indian family who owned a popular bakery just across the street from our house and I had played with Deanne often.

Although I had only seen her occasionally during the four years we were in Port of Spain, when I returned to Diego Martin, Deanne and I immediately became best friends again.

Chapter 3

Diego Martin: 11-18 years old

Diego Martin suited my sense of adventure. I could climb trees, make forts from the many coconut tree branches on our property, take walks up the river and set empty pans in strategic alcoves to catch those pretty multicolored fish called "millions." I was in heaven. I had miles of green spaces to explore with my dog and I had two sets of cousins who lived within walking distance. I was able to have a dog and two cats. I would go for long adventures up the river with my dog Jinxey. This was one of my favourite activities and for a destination I could also visit my cousins. It is surprising how much freedom I had. I could do whatever I wanted for hours at a time in those days.

During this period of my life, my mother's economic situation changed. Eric Williams, Trinidad's first prime minister after independence, dismantled the Anglo American Caribbean Commission shortly after he came into power in 1962. Prior to this, England had come to an agreement with the United States, giving them a 99-year lease of land at Chaguaramas, Trinidad. In addition to giving England some army destroyers, the U.S. set up research facilities for the Caribbean and Eric Williams was the main researcher. The focus of the research was the sociological, economic and political conditions in the Caribbean. Williams left the research facility to become the leader of the Peoples National Movement (PNM) in 1956.

After independence and coming to power, Williams and the PNM dismantled the Caribbean Commission. As a result, my mother was given a substantial settlement in U.S. dollars. Being the entrepreneur that she was, she used these funds to open a school supplies store on Warner Street in Port of Spain. This should have been an ideal location because many children walked along Warner Street to various schools in Port of Spain. Unfortunately, as many first time entrepreneurs find out, location is no guarantee of success. My mother's store folded after a year.

But my mother also had other prospects. She had a couple of other jobs before she opened a very successful business recruiting nurses and domestics to work in the United States. The parent company was in Baltimore, Maryland. Just before she opened the recruitment business, my mother sold Stanley Products to supplement her income. In the 1960's, Stanley products were high end household products that were sold by demonstration at parties, not unlike Tupperware, or Pampered Chef and similar products today. When my mother exhausted all her local friends and family with "Stanley parties," she branched out into other areas in Port of Spain such as Belmont and even Laventille, a notoriously poor and Black part of town. Parties were always after school so she often took me with her. I loved going with her when the parties were at our friends' houses, but the parties in Laventille were her most successful and had the biggest sales.

Alright, I admit it: I was a classist at this time in my life. Like many of my friends and family in Port of Spain at this time, I was embarrassed to go with my mother to these Laventille homes. Many years later in Canada, after my first son was born and I realized that babysitting, diapers and the other costs of a new baby would eliminate our vacation money, I started a gold jewelry business. After a day's work at the hospital as a dietitian, I would return home, play with my son, have a family dinner and then put my son to bed. At about eight o'clock, I would hire a babysitter and head out to host a jewelry party. It was a profitable side business. But I am telling you this story here because it bears so much similarity to my mother's. After I ran out of friends to have parties for me, I began to have parties in a subsidized housing unit. I was afraid that these mothers couldn't really afford gold jewelry. How wrong I was; they were my best customers! I remembered my mother in Laventille and saw the similarities and how far I had come.

No more false pride and, hopefully, no more classist attitudes.

My mother expected me to do well at school, but it was my brother who instilled the importance of further education. I was bright enough and didn't find schoolwork difficult. Classes were large, with as many as 40 kids in a class. My mother's only stipulation was that I had to come within the top 10 at the end of each school year. In Trinidadian schools at that time, all your marks were added up together at the end of the year, and you were ranked from first to last, e.g. 1-40, and your rank was posted on the bulletin board. I always easily made it into the top 10.

To get into the top secondary schools everyone in the island had to sit the "eleven plus" exams. Most families sent their children for extra tutoring to ensure they would get good marks. And yes, it was commonly understood that parents with lots of money could buy their children's admission to a better school. My mother didn't send me for additional tutoring. I would walk up the river to my cousins' home on a Saturday. Their grandmother would have them in lessons for most of the day. If I saw that they were doing school work, I would turn back and head home before their grandmother could see me and insist that I join my cousins in their schoolwork. I did not have any doubt that I would pass the "eleven plus" exams and gain admission to Bishop Anstey High School, which some of my cousins attended.

I could not believe it when the results came out. I passed the exams, but I did not gain admission to the high school I'd wanted;

I had to continue high school at Tranquility Girls, where I had gone to public school. I approached both my father and mother to send me to private school in Barbados. Barbadian private schools had all British teachers and were highly regarded. My mother said she didn't know what she would do without me if I went school in Barbados, but they both agreed that if that was what I wanted to do, they would try and arrange it.

Unfortunately for me, when I was twelve years old, my father died. I was very sad at the time. Because of his death, however, my idea to go to a private school in Barbados never came to fruition. It was at this time also that my brother had a serious talk with me about my future. He said that to continue to live the privileged life that I was living I would have to go to university and have a career. He put this in material terms and I was smart enough to understand what needed to be done. For the first time in my life I began to apply myself more.

This also coincided with my mother becoming stricter about school. This change came about not really because of needing the marks to attend university, but because at thirteen I became interested in boys. At fourteen I had a steady boyfriend. My mother set higher expectations for school so I would have more motivation to apply myself to schoolwork. Now I had to be in the top three in my class.

I had come within the top ten in public school, so being back at Tranquility with many of the brightest kids now at the three better high schools, it wasn't too difficult for me to achieve the new standards set by my mother. Between form one and five, I always came within the top three. At sixteen you had to take national departmental exams. These were the "External Examinations of the University of Cambridge" and they were posted to England to be corrected. A month later you would receive your results; not in private: they were posted in the national newspaper for everyone in the island to see! I passed my "O" levels (Ordinary) and was one of only three students to get a full certificate from Tranquility.

This meant that I would be able to go to Holy Name Convent to do my "A" levels (Advanced).

Immediately after puberty my tomboy days ended. I became interested in boys. I was always mature for my age and could converse with adults comfortably. Keep in mind that I had been my mother's confidante from an early age. At fourteen I met Phillip. He became my boyfriend and we continued to date until I left Trinidad to attend university in Canada. Phillip was five years older than me and was from a good family, meaning that our parents not only knew each other but my father's brother, my Uncle Dick, socialized with Phillip's parents.

I adored Phillip's dad, Uncle Parker. He would say to me, "You are the daughter I never had," and I believe his love for me was genuine. I idolized him for the father I did not grow up with. Auntie Evelyn, Phillip's mother, loved me as well. Many years later, when Phillip was married, she still said to me that she had been disappointed that Phillip and I didn't work out. Phillip belonged to the perfect family. Uncle Parker was a member of the yacht club and the family spent most weekends on their boat, going "down the islands." There were always friends around, music and partying. I learned to water ski and partied with them on many weekends. My mother felt it was a safe relationship since we spent so much time in the company of Phillip's parents.

My mother's main request was, "do not have sex before marriage, and do not get pregnant." She had worked too hard as a single mother rearing my brother and myself. If I became pregnant, she would be seen as an unfit mother. I would bring shame on her and the family. One other sub-rule was: no "parking." That was a time when many couples would park and neck, usually at the look-out on Lady Young Road just beyond the Hilton hotel.

I had no intention of having sex. I was determined to be a virgin on my wedding night. I was going to university and would have a career before getting married. My brother had convinced me that this was the best choice I could make. In Trinidad, as I suppose in many other countries, there were "good" girls and there were "bad" girls. Everyone knew which was which. Some girls had a reputation of going "all the way." There was even a double standard; many "good" girls did not mind if their boyfriends went all the way with the easy girls, because they weren't putting out themselves. Heavy necking, petting, even ejaculation were OK as long as there was no penetration. This was what I called doing "everything but."

My brother Edward left Trinidad for Edmonton, Alberta, Canada when I was sixteen. He was the first person in our family to choose Canada instead of England for further education. Edward had left home when I was fourteen to work at the Texaco oil refinery in Southern Trinidad as a student apprentice. At that time, they recruited high school graduates with their "A" levels to work as student apprentices. He lived with two sisters, the Cumberbatches, friends of my mother and aunts, in San Fernando. They had a huge, sprawling house and two dedicated maids who cooked and cleaned.

They treated my brother like family, with hot meals when he returned home after work and they did his laundry. Needless to say, he was quite comfortable with this arrangement. My brother presented himself as quite the playboy, driving a little convertible sports car for the commute from Port of Spain to San Fernando. Although my brother had his pick of girlfriends in Port of Spain within our tight circle of family and friends, it was in the South that he met Jean, the woman he would eventually marry, his life partner-to-be.

Jean was East Indian. Edward had always said he would marry an East Indian girl, and with Jean it appears he found his match. My mother and one of her best friends, Stella Jeffers, also East Indian, had had plans to match her daughter, Madge, with Edward. But both Edward and Madge both knew of this poorly kept secret and they patronized the two mothers by going on a few dates. Madge, an only child, was sent to finishing school in England, so Edward and Madge would only get together on her visits home. They were great friends, but never lovers. When things were getting serious with Jean, my brother wanted me to meet Jean's family and I was invited to Jean's home in Gasparillo, a part of the country I had never visited.

I was a bit surprised when I met Jean. She was a dark Indian with long hair. Her long hair was a feature my brother greatly admired. I had a great time on the visit, especially with Jean's mother. She cooked us roti and curry chicken in addition to a variety of wonderful Indian dishes. I went walking with her to the store and as we chatted, I realized how much she really liked my brother and approved of the match for her daughter.

Unfortunately this was not the case with Jean's eldest brother, Kelvin. Jean's father had passed away a few years before and her brother Kelvin thought it was his duty to take his place as head of the family, which included Jean and her three sisters. I only found out later that her brother was very much against Jean's relationship with Edward.

He would shout and yell at Jean when she returned home from a date with my brother.

The reasons for his objections included the fact that my brother was creole, i.e. mixed Black and European. It was also what Edward represented to Kelvin: a middle-class family from Port of Spain, the part of Trinidad that looked down on country folk. Kelvin said that he thought that my brother was only using Jean, that he would never marry her, and that even if their relationship resulted in marriage, it would never last. Today, Jean loves to point out how wrong Kelvin was. My brother and Jean recently celebrated their 50th wedding anniversary. Jean's two sisters, however, both of whom married East Indian husbands - with Kelvin's approval - did not have successful marriages.

I am going to relate an experience that I had at this time that, in retrospect, showed me that I possessed a strength I didn't know

I had; an experience that also defined me as an adult and helped me survive.

I was very shocked one day when I was late for my period. I typically had a very short cycle. My periods came every 24 days, regularly. To my surprise, at eighteen years old, a month before my "A" level exams, I missed my period. It was just 28 days - four days late. I was determined I wasn't going to have a shotgun marriage or have a baby at eighteen. I thought of my promise to my mother; I promised her that I wouldn't have sex. Although we didn't have penetration Phillip did ejaculate on top of me. I was going to University; I was going to follow my dreams - I had to have an abortion.

In Trinidad in the 1960's abortions were illegal. I told Phillip that he had to find a doctor who would perform an illegal abortion. I also had my final "A" level exams in a few weeks so it had to be done immediately. I would get half the money and he would get the other half. He found an abortionist and we were able to scrape up the exorbitant fee. He picked me up and drove me to a small house in Belmont. He waited in another room and I was made to lie down when a doctor and another guy whose house we were in, assisted the doctor with the procedure. No medication or anesthetic. He inserted a sharp object up my vagina; the pain was sudden and severe. It was over in minutes. The bed was soaked in blood. I was given double pads to wear. Phillip drove me home. I bled daily. To this day I do not know how I continued to study and sit my exams. I was weak and tired all the time. My mother knew that I had heavy periods so she really didn't notice that I was bleeding daily. I lost about 15 pounds. Thank goodness for exams. Most family and friends assumed that my weight loss was from the stress I was going through, studying long hours.

After exams my boyfriend and I were very worried. I was still bleeding a month after my butchering. My bleeding went on and off again for two more months! In retrospect, I do not even know if I was really pregnant; I was only ten days late when the abortion occurred. Stress of exams or a miscalculation could have happened. The point is I couldn't chance it. I had to sit my exams on time and I had worked too hard to get into Holy Name Convent; I would be letting too many people down, including myself. But the greatest pain would have been the hurt and disappointment on my mother's face and in her heart if she had found out. I know all the other adults in my life would have suggested that Phillip and I get married. My dear mother had worked so hard to provide my brother and me with a comfortable middle-class upbringing. I would be seen as one of "those girls." I had promised her. I wanted her to be proud of me. There was also my extended family; so many people. I would not tell anyone, ever. I swore Phillip to secrecy also.

It was about thirty years later before I told anyone what had happened. The person told was my brother. I told him also about Sleepy so he could know that my adolescence and young adulthood had challenges and hardships that he could not have imagined that I had experienced. These were hidden secrets that I had kept for decades and if they didn't define me, they were definitely part of who I was and I think part of what has contributed to my strength, values and perseverance in adulthood.

I wrote my exams in early June 1969. My bleeding from the abortion stopped by the end of July. While I waited for my results from England I felt that I could begin to enjoy the summer. High school days were over, and I was confident that I had passed my examinations. I began to look forward to a summer of parties with friends, going to Maracas beach, water skiing down the islands, and just beach bumming around. My mother knew how hard I had worked and was pleased that I had started to be happy again. She had picked up on my stress of the past couple months but she blamed that on my exams.

As far as we all thought, I would be heading to the University of the West Indies in Trinidad in September along with most of my school friends. The only problem with this plan was the fact that my older brother Edward saw my future a bit differently. He had convinced me to apply to Canada for my landed immigrant status a few months before, which I did. He wanted me to attend the University of Alberta where he was in his third year in Engineering. My brother in his thorough way had researched the point system that Canada used for accepting landed immigrants. I had the right education and enough money because both my grandmother and my great-aunt, Tantie Vie, had each left me $1000 in their wills. That would be worth at least $15,000 in today's dollars. Edward had even arranged for a friend to write a letter saying that I had a job in his company – okay it wasn't true, but it made my application stronger. Edward was coming home for a visit and coincidentally, I received an invitation to an interview at the Canadian embassy during Edward's visit. He brought piles of information on Canada and life there for me to review. I got ready for the interview with the same fervor I gave to exam preparation.

My interview went well. I received my acceptance as a landed immigrant to Canada at about the same time that my examination results came in from England. I had passed all my subjects with flying colors. Then the rush started! I had to try to make it up to Canada by September for the beginning of University. As it turns out, I didn't arrive until early October. My brother said that was OK: I could work for the rest of the year and begin to save the money I would need for university.

Leaving my mother was the hardest thing I ever did. I could not imagine life without her. I had slept with my mother most of my life. It was just when I was sixteen and started "A" levels at Holy Name Convent, that I thought I should break myself of the habit. I moved into my own bedroom. It was my brother's old room, a quiet room with a big desk making it easier to study. I would fall asleep at the wee hours of the morning, my glasses still on and a book on my chest. My mother was diabetic and would routinely get up at three in the morning to go to the bathroom. On her way back from the bathroom, she would most often check on me, take my glasses off, rest my book down and occasionally she would climb into the single bed with me. So we still slept together sometimes.

I was also concerned about my mother's health. She had lost a lot of weight and had to drive into Port of Spain every morning to get an insulin shot. At eighteen years old I didn't understand diabetes or how to help her. All I knew was she shouldn't have sweets and desserts made with sugar, but whenever I pointed this out to my mother, she would discount my comments saying she would die happy eating whatever she wanted. In 1969 I didn't know how ill my mother really was, I wouldn't have left Trinidad if I had understood.

I knew that I would miss my extended family, especially my two aunts and my dear aunty Milly. Another person I would miss was Mary, our maid and my nanny. She had become my friend and confidante before I left Trinidad; Mary, who did everything for me. During my last days at home after "A" levels, she spoilt me even more than usual. I would lie in bed reading on rainy days and Mary would make whatever I wanted to eat and bring it up to my bedroom for me. It was on one of these occasions that I promised to bring her up to Canada to look after me. She gave me the sweetest smile. Neither of us knew how unrealistic this promise was, but it was comforting and a way of saying goodbye.

Chapter 4

Immigration to Canada: Edmonton, Alberta, 1969-70

I arrived in Canada in October, 1969. I was so naive. My life growing up in Trinidad had been pretty idyllic. I was indulged by an extensive family, popular with my many friends, and sheltered from the rest of the world; sheltered as well from the rest of the island. Although I knew Port of Spain and the north of the island, I did not know the rest of the island. As I have since learned, having returned numerous times to visit other parts of Trinidad, central and south Trinidad were either predominantly Black or East Indian. Each area has its own history, its own culture, and forms part of the whole history and culture of Trinidad and Tobago.

In my part of Trinidad, I had everything that I wanted growing up; why would I ever want to leave? My brother's reasons for wanting me to immigrate to Canada were more than just so I could attend university. He wanted me to "grow up" and experience the "real" world and enjoy opportunities I could never have back home.

My brother's fiancée, Jean, had moved to Edmonton from Ottawa in 1969. She had immigrated just after my brother, but initially she moved to Ottawa where her boss at Texaco in Trinidad had arranged a job for her with a colleague there. She then moved to Edmonton prior to my arrival. My brother arranged that I would share an apartment with Jean. As I have said, I arrived too late to begin university, so I set out to find my first real job, and work for a year before beginning my courses.

I had excellent marks in my "A" levels, the equivalent of grade 13 in Canada, and a bookkeeping certificate. I applied for many office clerical jobs but received no offers. This was my first wake-up call. One gentleman summed it up for me. It was a tiny Kodak counter. The job was simple: you needed a pretty smile, needed to be polite, and be able to use a cash register. The owner Mr. Insley took my hand and said, "You seem to be a lovely, person, and bright, but I still can't hire you because you are colored. I know my customers wouldn't buy here anymore. I'd lose my business."

Well, at least he was straight with me; he put it into words and confirmed my feelings; he told me why I had received all my rejections: my brown face. Being colored/mixed race, part Black would always be a hurdle to my getting ahead in Canada. At this time, in Canada, of course, there was actually no mixed race or colored; there was Black and white, us and them. All people of color were "them." I thanked Mr. Insley. I rushed out of his store and headed for a bus bench down the street and sobbed. I wondered if there was any sense in continuing to read the want ads. In my head, I think I heard my mother's voice saying, 'Don't give up." So I read some more want ads. Maybe a dress store would hire me?

At least if I worked at a dress store I wouldn't have to take any of the terrible part-time jobs I had worked at for a while. For a brief time I worked for Henderson's Directory and canvassed door-to-door in Edmonton. I had fond memories of canvassing but I didn't make any money. I was paid a few cents for each card I filled out. This was in a part of Edmonton where many older people lived. It was also in the winter, so often they would open the door to this half frozen girl from the islands and invite me in for a cup of hot chocolate. (I didn't drink coffee or tea, both adult drinks to me at this time). I was brought up to be polite so I usually accepted the offer. In some cases I would spend up to a half-hour chatting with these lonely souls who were very interested in my story of growing up in the islands. For a brief time, I also did telemarketing, selling hockey tickets over the phone. I never wanted to do either of those jobs again!

I remembered back to Trinidad when I was younger. At the time, my brother thought I should get a job over the holidays in Port of Spain to get some pocket money. He argued that instead of me asking my mother or my aunts for money, whenever I needed it, I should get a job and earn my pocket money. I was alarmed: "Me, sell in a store?" I said. "Never!" None of my close friends would even consider working at a store. But my brother had such an influence on my extended family that his suggestion resulted in a family conference. My mother, my two aunts and the matriarch, great-aunt Tantie Vie, came up with a solution. I would make pastels and sell them.

Pastels are Venezuelan delicacies that are very popular in Trinidad. Many people made and sold pastels as a cottage industry. Tantie Vie even made a budget for me that would give me a 50% profit. Fifteen dollars for supplies and fifteen dollars profit. I would make one hundred pastels for sale at thirty cents each that would bring in thirty dollars. Of course my mother indulged me by letting me keep the full thirty dollars. She didn't take out her share for supplies.

Even though my great school marks, my intelligence and many family and friend contacts, would have gotten me any number of clerical jobs in Trinidad, they did not hold the same weight in Canada where I had absolutely no contacts. I had to face this. It had been almost a month since I had arrived, and I had received so many refusals. I determined I would work selling in a store. Of course, out of embarrassment I wouldn't say anything about my foray into retail sales to my family back home. I saw that a sales clerk was needed at D'Allaird's, a dress store that I had seen many times on Jasper Avenue, a few blocks away. I carefully filled out an application form and to my surprise I was granted an interview immediately.

The manager, Mrs. Higgins, a kind elderly lady, began to ask me questions that were very different from my previous interviews. I had read a few pamphlets from Canada Manpower, a national government employee support agency, and also a couple of library books on how to prepare for an interview. That day, however, my mind was too filled with Mr. Insley's comments to think of saying the right thing. Mrs. Higgins continued her gentle questioning and then came around the desk to me, put her arm around my shoulder and asked, "Getting a job has been difficult, hasn't it?"

I looked up into her kind face and began to sob. Through tears, I explained all the frustrations and the silent prejudice I had experienced. I left her office actually feeling good to have met one person who had empathized with me. But I knew I had blown the interview and wouldn't be hired. Much to my surprise, early the next morning, I got a call asking me to report to work at 9 o'clock sharp.

So I was off to a real job! I was now a full-time sales clerk at D'Allairds, working in a new boutique they had opened that would attract a younger clientele. From day one, I worked with Yvonne, who was about twenty-five years old, and also Jane, a teenager like me who worked part-time on weekends and after school. Jane was from a middleclass family and apparently lived in a big home. Her parents were members of a club with an indoor swimming pool and Jane was planning a party there.

All Yvonne and I heard about were her party plans. She was friendly to me but I realized as time went on that I wouldn't be even considered as a friend she would invite to her party. She saw me as a Black immigrant who wasn't in her parents' economic class. In my mind I reminisced about just a few months before when I spent my weekends attending similar parties in Trinidad.

Mr. Jones, the gentleman I worked for part time selling hockey tickets, was polite to my brother and congratulated me when I told him I had gotten a job working at a dress store. My brother had taken me to see Mr. Jones that evening to collect the few dollars I had made the previous week. His office was a walk-up apartment on Jasper Avenue, a very poor area of downtown Edmonton which sex workers frequented. I understood that this was their only way of survival and making a living; my heart went out to them. My job selling hockey tickets had been an evening job. After work I had to carefully make my way through the sex workers on the sidewalks of Jasper Avenue, trying not to be accosted myself.

When we left Mr. Jones' room and got into my brother's car, he hugged me very close for a while. I began to cry and thought of my mother. I think Edward was thinking of my mother also. My brother never understood or experienced the rejections I did. He had two main jobs in Edmonton. He worked at a halfway house for delinquent boys. He was perfect for that job and I am sure he got it because of who he was: a six-foot Black guy who could manhandle any of the boys who were aggressive. His summer job was working for a big oil company, Amoco, who had specifically recruited engineering students from his program at the University of Alberta.

I had to try to understand this new country that I had come to. I turned to books and stumbled upon some written by West Indian authors. They answered some of my questions about immigrants from the Caribbean who had left there before me and had experienced similar prejudices. The books were from the *Caribbean Writers Series*. These books gave vivid examples of prejudice and class differences experienced by West Indians, most of whom had immigrated to England. Samuel Selvon in his book, *The Lonely Londoners* describes a variety of Caribbean immigrants who had left the islands for London after the Second World War looking for a better life. They expected to be welcomed by the country they had fought for. Instead they faced racism, harsh weather and unemployment. They survived by banding together. George Lamming's *The Pleasures of Exile* echoed these sentiments. Many of these books made me stronger, they reinforced that what I was experiencing was real and not something that I was doing wrong. My innocent teenage eyes were opening to the battle that lay ahead. I had to have a plan.

I had completed history at "A" levels in Trinidad. I studied British and European history. I realized I knew next to nothing about West Indian history. I recognized myself as a West Indian in many of the books I was reading and I realized also that like many of the characters in these stories, the reactions that I was experiencing in Canada were based on ignorance and stereotypes. My main challenge would be to get people to know me and hopefully get past the stereotypes. I realized that I would need to approach this strategy one person at a time. That was all that I could hope for. There would be Canadians who wanted to stay behind the glass partition; I could do nothing about them. The best thing for me to do would be to minimize those experiences.

My brother shared a story with me about an exit interview he had with his manager at Amoco after his summer job. The manager was a white American. He complimented my brother on the exceptional job he had done that summer. He also wanted to share with him that he admired that whenever they interacted, my brother approached him as an equal, and asked intelligent questions directly. My brother wasn't sure exactly what point he was making and asked for clarification. His manager explained that he had only worked with American Blacks before. They approached him in a subservient way and Edward did not.

My brother, rightly I think, said that he thought American Blacks had been conditioned for generations to be deferential to whites. They were so accustomed to that relationship towards whites - no eye contact, white man as boss - that even some of the Blacks from his University still had some of this self-image in their psyche and behaviour. This behaviour was also a built-in protective mechanism that was learned by American Blacks; appearing too "uppity" was threatening to some white Americans, so why risk it? As my brother related this story, I realized that like my brother, I didn't project this attitude of subservience either. I saw stereotyping as ignorance on the part of the person who was responding to me that way. Our experiences of growing up in Trinidad, a more integrated society, meant that we had not learned that deferential behaviour. Little did I know or realize at this time that this way of thinking would be an obstacle to my employment in the future.

When I reflected on this more, I realized that class had as much to do with this behaviour as color did; that this was how poor, working class people in Trinidad - whether they were Black, creole, colored or East Indian - reacted to me. Our handyman, dear Joseph, who had looked after our family for years doing gardening, repairs and any odd jobs, changed to calling me Miss Cecily when I came into my teens. It made me sad at the time, but I knew it was what everyone expected and I didn't have the words to change it or even address the unfairness. I know now that it was economic and class-related in Trinidad. Everyone knew their place in the sixties, although this differential behavior does not exist to the same extent today. You knew to respect anyone who was in a position higher than you. I understood at an early age that I had internalized the unfairness and injustice of racialized behaviour, and my middle-class upbringing had not required me to be deferential to whites. At that point, I realized that most of the Canadians I had met so far were ignorant about life in the Caribbean and Trinidad in particular. If they thought about us at all, they saw us all as poor immigrants who were not in their class. If I wanted to be accepted in Canada for who I was, and not as a stereotype, I would have to change that attitude one person at a time.

I was enjoying my job at D'Allairds. The staff were older women, for the most part, who approached me in a motherly way, and were always inquiring how I was getting along. Mrs. Higgins in particular, kept her eyes on me and would invite me into her office to chat from time to time. She would be the first of many managers that would be of assistance to me in the job market.

I do have some fun memories from Edmonton. One was experiencing my first Halloween. I volunteered to take the two girls that lived in the upstairs apartment trick or treating. We went from house to house in our neighbourhood. They were both dressed up as fairy princesses. I was excited to take part, so my sister-in-law put a little extra makeup on me and dressed me up to look like a gypsy. We went to each door yelling, "Trick or treat!" I could not believe all the chocolates and candies we received! Although I was the adult walking the kids from door to door, many people would encourage me to choose some candy. I guess at nineteen I was just a teenager and looked like one of the kids.

Another very special event was my first snowfall. I ran outside without a coat and twirled around catching this cold, white fluff falling from heaven. In Trinidad, we have two seasons: the wet season and the dry season. The temperature variance between seasons, or even between night and day is not usually more than ten degrees Fahrenheit, that is between eighty and ninety degrees. In Canada winter would become my favorite season, summer a close second.

I had read many books as a child and one was an adventure series of two close friends at a boarding school in Switzerland. They had tremendous winter adventures, solving all sorts of mysteries. When I had wanted to go away to high school, I mentioned Switzerland to my parents. This of course was immediately discounted. At twelve I had no concept of how expensive – and impossible - a request like this was. But my first Canadian winter reminded me of reading those books about Switzerland.

My brother, Edward, and his fiancée, Jean, actually began skiing that winter. They were able to go with a small university group on weekends. I really envied them but I knew I couldn't afford it. It would be a dream I would save for the future.

My brother did give me a pair of ice skates that first Christmas in Canada. There was another West Indian friend that I would go ice-skating with on a lake near our home. I skated immediately without falling down too often. I couldn't master how to stop though! Perhaps, this had to do with all my roller-skating; I used to roller-skate all over Port of Spain in Trinidad. Skating made me enjoy the winter and appreciate the cold weather. It was a serene feeling, gliding around in this open space, often with no one else around to break into my quiet thoughts.

Another outdoor winter activity that I got to experience that first winter was tobogganing. I did this with Mary, the niece of the lady, Leela, who lived upstairs. Mary was from a big family with two brothers and two sisters, all younger than her. Mary came to stay with Leela one day because of a problem that occurred at Mary's home. Leela told us the story; her dad had inappropriately touched poor Mary. It was near Christmas and Mary would be visiting her family's home in the outskirts of Edmonton for the weekend. She invited me to come on her visit home with her. Against my brother's objections, I was determined to go. My existence so far had been going back and forth to work, reading, and looking at our black and white TV when I got home.

That Saturday morning after breakfast, Mary and her brothers and sisters and I headed down to this hill where we tobogganed all morning. We managed to avoid hitting any trees and we would either go fast enough to bounce over a frozen creek at the bottom or roll off the sled just before we reached the creek. I can say that tobogganing reminded me of my tomboy days in Trinidad. Tobogganing was exhilarating; the speed produced a feeling of danger that was thrilling, not frightening. We laughed a lot and had a blast! It was sad returning home.

The apartment that Jean and I lived in was a basement apartment in a small house. Leela lived upstairs on the main floor with her two children, Molly and Suzie. They were only seven and four and I adored them. I would spoil them with candy from time to time. My brother studied during the week but would come over every Sunday. He would usually cook this great Sunday meal; baked stuffed chicken, Trinidadian style, or roast beef or pork, well-seasoned just like my mother's. We would often have a drink of Trinidadian rum and coke with supper. My sister-in-law still laughs at how tipsy we would both get after just one drink and how we would laugh ourselves silly.

I love my sister-in-law and she loves me. For this to have remained the case after living with me in Edmonton says a lot about her loving character. I had arrived in Canada not being able to cook; I had never had to prepare a full meal - or taken any responsibility for housework. In Trinidad, it was all done for me. As I mentioned, every middle-class family had at least one maid and sometimes two or three. Upper-class families had even more "help."

On weekends, Jean and I took turns sharing the cleaning of our little apartment. It was about the third time that it was my turn to clean the bathroom, that Jean approached me and said, "I notice you didn't clean the toilet." This just consisted of pouring some toilet cleaner in and swishing it around with the toilet brush. When she asked me why I didn't clean the toilet on my cleaning days, I said, "Do I have to?" The logic of being so scornful about cleaning a toilet that we were the only ones using, shows me how much I had to learn.

That Christmas presented a dilemma for me. Christmas was by far my favorite time of year. My memories were of the many bazaars to attend, presents to buy and wrap and Christmas trees to decorate. Our trees in Trinidad were big branches in the shape of a Christmas tree sprayed silver or gold. Decorations were usually glass balls, most often imported from the United States or brought back by family or friends who visited abroad. I wanted to send Christmas presents to Trinidad for my family. I had been so indulged with presents for Christmas back home that I wanted to give back. I was working, but I didn't have any extra money for gifts. Just before Christmas I saw an advertisement in the newspaper for extra postal workers over the Christmas holidays to sort the many parcels they received. I applied and got the job. I thought my problem had been solved.

I worked from midnight to six A.M. at the post office. After finishing my shift at D'Allaird's, I would rush home, have supper, a short nap and then head out for my midnight shift at the post office. After that shift, I would return home, have another little rest, eat breakfast, and then head to D'Allairds for ten. The Christmas rush at the post office covered three weeks. Although I didn't get as much sleep as I should have, I counted all the extra money I had received. There was more than enough to buy presents for everyone! I think back and reflect about this experience, one which I have repeated many times in my life, and I know I am just following my mother's example. When she had any financial woes, she just worked harder and found something else she could do to earn a little extra.

Despite making a few friends, I was lonely in Edmonton, and unhappy. I didn't see why I would want to stay here. I wanted to go back to Trinidad. I dreamed about what I had left: my mother, family and friends who saw me as bright and intelligent. I could go to university in Trinidad and have a career there as well. Why shouldn't I return? I posed this possibility to my brother. He objected immediately: it would be giving up. I did not need to burden my mother, who would feel responsible for looking after me. As it turned out, my mother was not well. My brother had been shocked when he had seen her a few months earlier in Trinidad. Her diabetes was ravaging her; she had lost weight, and her blood sugars were always out of control. My aunts didn't say much in their letters, but I could read between the lines. In my mother's last letter to me, she didn't write in a straight line and my Aunt Milly finished the letter for her, her eyesight was failing, one of the many complications of her diabetes. I accepted my brother's advice and realized I couldn't go back home.

I pondered this problem. I had spent a week in Toronto with my best friend Deanne, who had immigrated to Canada two years before me. She took me clubbing and to a couple of parties. I had met some of her friends and she had a good job working as a secretary at the Ontario Institute for Studies in Education, at the University of Toronto. She lived in an apartment with her English friend, Jackie. Perhaps Toronto could be my solution. I thought if I could move to Toronto, Deanne would let me crash at her apartment until I found a job. Remember, Deanne was my best friend since I was four years old; we were inseparable then and I had every confidence she would welcome me with open arms and be willing to help me out in any way she could.

When I told my brother my plan he wasn't supportive. "What about my plans for you to go to the University of Alberta?" he said. He also thought that Alberta's economy was better than Ontario's. He sent me to the library to research this. I did. All my research proved that my brother was right. Alberta was richer than Ontario. It was wealthier and accommodation was less expensive. At that time, Alberta really did seem to be a place of more opportunity. But I also knew that Alberta wasn't for me. I told my brother, "You are right, but I am still moving to Toronto." I talked with Deanne and she was good with letting me stay with her until I was settled. Deanne welcomed me as a best friend would. So after six months in Western Canada, I was on my way east to Toronto.

Chapter 5

Toronto, Ontario, 1970 - 1972

Upon my arrival in Toronto, my first goal was to get a job so I could pay my share for food and rent. I had learned a lot in Edmonton. All the job advertisements wanted "Canadian experience" which I only had in retail. I didn't want to continue to work in retail. I needed to have experience other than that. My mother, who now had her own company recruiting nurses and domestics to the United States, was my answer. I was in survival mode. I got my mother to produce an excellent reference under her company name of my having performed a variety of clerical duties. This was not totally untrue. Although unpaid, I had sometimes assisted my mother with filing and sorting out applicants.

The next step was to find a clerical job that didn't include typing. The want ads appeared to have the perfect job: working for Eaton's in their market research division, for three researchers who were investigating the feasibility of a very big project: the Eaton's Centre. The advertised job was for doing graphs and percentages using a calculator. This would be a piece of cake, right? I could do percentages in my head, but using a calculator ….. what was a calculator?

I was familiar with a slide rule but not a calculator. I phoned up a Trinidad friend, Ian, who described a calculator to me. In

1970 a calculator was this big machine, as big as a large typewriter, with numbers zero to nine. You punched in your numbers and pulled a lever to calculate additions, subtractions and percentages. I visualized the calculator and I decided that any machine that added, subtracted and did percentages was definitely one I could master. I went to the interview with the manager, Bruce Wilson. He offered me the job on the spot. It had been less than a week since I arrived in Toronto and I would start my new job on Monday.

I arrived bright and early. My senior co-worker, Jackie, was responsible for showing me the ropes. Jackie sat with a pile of papers, took the one on top and began to punch in figures on the calculator without looking at the keys. She did this just like typing, by touch. I was alarmed. I would have to look at the keys to punch in the numbers and I couldn't do it by touch. I sat down at my desk situated in front of Jackie. She would be able to see that I wasn't using touch. In the first couple minutes I quickly ran over my options: I could confess that I hadn't seen a calculator until a few minutes ago or I could fake it. I decided on the latter. I punched the numbers as fast as I could, looking at the keyboard. Jackie said nothing. Before break I took my pile of calculations to her, she praised me for completing them so quickly. I was okay. I was hired in my first clerical job. Thank you, Toronto!

I didn't tell Bruce Wilson that I had plans to go to university in September; I didn't think I would be hired to any full-time job for just a few months. So I set out to investigate my options. The point is I didn't know what I wanted to study at university. All the programs I had been looking at with my brother for the University of Alberta were geared to accounting or business, nothing I was really interested in. In my teens, I had thought of being a psychologist. I think anyone who has gone through divorced parents thinks that they can fix things for people who were going through similar experiences.

I had a discussion with my brother about my choices. He didn't think that business was a good choice because it was a male field; what would I do if I got married and wanted time off when I got pregnant? I then suggested psychology and he said psychology wasn't a "bread and butter" career; besides, I would need at least a master's degree to work in psychology. I went to the University of Toronto to pick up a calendar that listed every degree program they offered. I read the calendar from cover to cover and found a degree that suited me perfectly: nutrition and food.

I was a health nut at that time, along with Deanne. We would buy carrot juice from Rolly's on Yonge Street every day; we frequented health food stores, had read Adelle Davis' books, *Let's Get Well* and *Let's Eat Right to Keep Fit*, in addition to *Diet for a Small Planet* by Frances Moore Lappe. I knew enough science and logic to know that the health food books I had read weren't always scientific. So I was excited at the thought of attending university to learn the science of nutrition. I was very idealistic about what I would do with my degree. I thought that I would become a writer about nutrition for the everyday person.

I had only been in Toronto for three months when my brother announced that he and Jean would be getting married in June that year and they wanted me to return to Edmonton for their wedding. I said I couldn't afford the trip as I would have to dip into my savings for university the following year. My mother was distraught that I would even consider not attending my brother's wedding. She was going to make the trip against her doctor's advice. She would first fly to Toronto and then continue onto Edmonton with me. I had no choice at that point so I made plans for the trip with her. When I met my mother at Pearson airport in Toronto, I received a shock.

I first saw my mother at the other side of a glass petition. I called out her name. She recognized my voice but couldn't see me. Her sight had deteriorated even more. She was walking with a cane because she had an infected foot, a result of the lack of circulation in her lower extremities. She had neglected a cut and it had gone septic. In spite of her health, this was an exciting time for my mother. Her son had graduated from the University of Alberta with an engineering degree and he was getting married. I wanted to share in her happiness. I was their only bridesmaid; I was happy I had made the trip back.

A year later, in August of 1971, I received a call from my two aunts, my mother's sisters. I had to come to Trinidad immediately. My mother had been admitted to hospital in a diabetic coma. She was not expected to live very long. I flew to Trinidad immediately. I rushed to the hospital as soon as I arrived. My mother had regained some consciousness that day; she recognized my voice but couldn't reply to me coherently. A day later I went to visit her doctor to discuss her prognosis. He explained kidney failure to me. Although she was out of her coma, she was dying. In Canada there was dialysis, but this wasn't available in Trinidad in 1971. She had only weeks or a few months to live. I spent every day at her side loving her as best as I could. There was nothing I could do to save her. I didn't want to return to Canada. I wanted to stay in Trinidad with my mother.

My mother had heard me say that I wasn't returning to Canada, and despite her weak state, she asked to speak to my Uncle Parker. She knew that I loved and respected his opinion and she asked him to convince me to return to Canada. He told me she said that she had worked so hard to see me succeed. She was proud of what I had accomplished and for that reason she wanted me to return to Canada to attend university, not to stay in Trinidad. She had accepted she was dying and my staying in Trinidad could not change that. Her loving sisters would look after her. I cried myself to sleep that night, for all the things my mother wouldn't be there for: the completion of my degree, my first job as a dietitian, my marriage and the birth of her grandchildren.

Both her sisters lived long enough to see my achievements for her. My mother died in December 1971, a few months after I left Trinidad. I had just turned twenty-one years old. I was officially an orphan. My brother also flew to Trinidad. He arrived the same day I left in September. He and Jean had left Edmonton and just moved to Ithaca, New York, so Edward could attend Cornell University where he had a scholarship to complete his MBA. As soon as Jean was settled, he took the next flight to Trinidad. He was lucky: my mother was discharged from hospital and he described doing my favorite thing, lying with her and giving her comfort.

I had applied to the University of Toronto to begin university in September 1971. I was told, however, that I was missing a prerequisite subject for studying nutrition: grade 13 chemistry. Undaunted, I signed up at the Jarvis Collegiate Night School to take grade 13 chemistry starting in the fall of 1971 and winter of 1972. Everyone thought that I should take at least grade 12 - or even grade 11 - chemistry before I took it at the grade 13 level. I was very confident, however, about my ability to understand any subject once I put my mind to it. So I enrolled at Jarvis Collegiate to take grade 13 chemistry as well as calculus and English literature. Of course, I was working full time and I was living with three other girls who usually started partying on Thursday night and didn't stop until Sunday. I had to devise a system of studying.

I lived on St Mary's Street near Bloor and Yonge. My office at Eaton's was at Yonge and Queen, a half-hour walk from my apartment. I would carefully set up a chapter from one of my courses to memorize on my way to work. After overcoming my initial difficulty with using a calculator, I began to find that my job at Eaton's was easy to do. Because I could do math in my head, I was able to finish my calculations in half the time the other clerks were taking. So I devised a method to use some of my time at work to complete my school work. I chose to do English literature at night school because of my love of reading and I was excited to study modern books like Arthur Miller's *Death of a Salesman*. In Trinidad we had a nun choose our literature books and she often had a predilection for medieval tragedies – painful! Arthur Miller was a welcome relief.

I passed all three subjects at Jarvis Collegiate with A's. That resulted in my being accepted at both the University of Toronto and the University of Guelph for September 1972. I chose University of Guelph because I had to move out of Toronto if I planned to get any studying done. This wasn't night school anymore.

Toronto was a great, safe city in the early '70's. I lived with three other girls in our two-bedroom apartment in downtown Toronto on St. Mary's street at Bloor and Yonge. You could walk everywhere from this address. We spent our spare time "liming" and going to lots of parties. Our apartment was a party apartment, which was always filled with friends. You actually felt safe walking the streets of Toronto late at night back then. We partied all weekend starting from Thursday night. We knew all the neighbourhoods and apartment buildings famous for throwing big parties. If we weren't invited to a party on the weekend, we would head to a party apartment, count the floors with loud music and just show up. We would choose a name like "John" and say he invited us. Even if there wasn't a John, no one would ask four attractive girls to leave. I dated a variety of different people. One of my longer relationships was with Peter Pfeiffer, a Swiss citizen who was working and living in Toronto and saving for a long trip through the United States before he returned home to Switzerland. I visited him in Switzerland in the summer of 1972 before I attended university. I also hung out with a West Indian crowd, mainly Trinidadian, and briefly dated an East Indian Trinidadian.

My last boyfriend in Toronto was Mike, a white Canadian schoolteacher, six years older than I was. He was intelligent and mature and we spent time discussing politics and social issues of the day but not race. Mike lived in my building and we were back and forth to each other's apartments. It was after the news of the death of my mother in December 1971 that I took Mike's offer to stay at his place for some comfort. It was that night that I lost my virginity. Officially, Mike didn't know that I was a virgin, and I didn't tell him.

In Canada, I had learned that you were either white or Black. There was no in-between. And I was okay with that. I was beginning to develop a Black consciousness. I was able to maneuver through most of the color roadblocks that I encountered. In my two years in Toronto I really didn't run into much overt prejudice. As I have come to understand, Toronto didn't see Blacks as a "problem" until the mid-seventies. Before then there were still a relatively small number of Blacks in Toronto; we fell under the radar. In 1971 Statistics Canada reported 34,400 Blacks in Ontario, Quebec, Nova Scotia and New Brunswick, this number increased to 239,500 by 1982, a jump from 0.2% to 1.0% of the total population, a 5-fold increase.

One of the things I had learned in Trinidad was that it was the colored Trinidadians (lighter-skinned, less mixed - the ones who "could pass for white") who displayed the most prejudice towards darker coloreds (browner-skinned, more obviously mixed). In Canada at this time, the groups who were striving for acceptance by the white Anglo-Saxon majority, and who were the focus of ethnic prejudice, were the Italians and Eastern Europeans. As the Italians and the Eastern Europeans became more integrated, however, it was the Blacks from the West Indies and from Africa, who were the next largest immigrant group, and they became the focus of white racism.

This was clearly seen in the handling of the Montreal computer riots at Sir George Williams University in January of 1969, just before I came to Canada. As you know there are always two sides to any story but in my assessment, this story was about clear, covert racism that was discounted. The incident started with a complaint that one computer professor consistently gave lower grades to West Indian Black students. There were many examples but one that was blatantly obvious was when a white student copied word for word his Black partner's lab report and was given a higher grade for the same report. In spite of a complaint to administration, these students were ignored and accused of whining and inappropriately expressing dissatisfaction with lower grades.

When this incident was written up in the student newspaper, *The Georgian*, it received support from many white students who joined Black students and approached administration, again to no avail. It was after this long process of not being heard that both white and Black students occupied the computer labs. Negotiations continued but broke down and the riot police were called. A fire broke out. There is a discrepancy of who started the fire. The police say that it was the students and the students blame the police, arguing why would we start a fire when we were barricaded in the lab ourselves? I am relating this story for you to understand what happened next. The crowd watching the fire chanted, "Let the niggers burn." As the students inside escaped the flames, they were subjected to savage beatings. Of 1044 charges only 9 were upheld. Public opinion was against the students who were described as criminals, thugs and anarchists.

What I want to point out is a theme that I have described before. West Indians from middle-class backgrounds expect to be treated equally to whites and when they are not they will stand up for equal treatment. Several of the students involved in the Sir George Williams riots were from privileged families in the Caribbean. For example, Roosevelt Douglas, who later became Prime Minister of Dominica, Anne Cools, who was the first Black member of the Canadian Senate, and Joey Jagan, Jr., the son of a Guyanese prime minister. There was overt racism in this event as well as many microaggressions, covert in nature, in the handling of this incident. Reading about this was a learning experience for me. In future, I would have to pick my battles carefully.

There are two incidents that I now want to share. I had one incident with an Italian girlfriend, Angelina, with whom I often had coffee breaks at Eaton's. We talked about food and recipes. I loved Italian food and one day Angelina invited me home for dinner. Her father had passed away about a year before and she lived in a small house in the west end of Toronto with her mother and her sister. I believe that my girlfriend was the bread winner of the family. Her mother looked after the house and cooked meals for the family. Angelina told her mother that she was bringing a friend home for supper. We walked into the living room. Her mother, all dressed in black because she was still mourning her husband's death two years before, came in from the kitchen and saw me. She didn't speak much English but I can recognize profanity in any language. She screamed at me to "get out, esci, negra" waving her hands, I exited quickly and took the subway home. Back at work the next day, neither Angelina nor I spoke about the incident. Neither of us had the words. I knew she was embarrassed. Incidents like this were highly offensive, but I ascribed them to ignorance and tried to move on.

My other significant incident was with a friend Nick, from my calculus night classes at Jarvis Collegiate. He had a crush on me but I thought he was too young. He was my age but I had always dated boys who were older than me. He wasn't doing well in calculus. He had failed it in high school and needed a good mark to apply to university. I agreed to tutor him. He gave me his telephone number and I phoned to set up a time. His mother answered the phone and picked up on my West Indian accent. She shouted at me in her broken English, "Leave my son alone, don't call him. He no date a negro."

I guess I could have refused to help Nick. Instead I never told him about his mother's outburst. He was so far behind it was a lost cause; he then asked me if he could choose the seat behind me at our final exams, and if I would let him copy my answers. I thought, what the heck, he seemed like a nice person, so I let him. If he got caught he would be in trouble, not me. He didn't get caught. I got an A in calculus and Nick got a B. He was elated. Would you believe, seven years later I bumped into him on Yonge

Street in Toronto? He had just been accepted into Law at the University of Toronto. We got together for a meal and reminisced about our friendship years earlier.

There were a few other racial incidents, but by then I had learned to avoid putting myself in situations where I might be compromised. One small incident that did alarm me, however, happened on Yonge Street where I was watching a parade. After an hour watching the parade, I had to pee! My white girlfriend and I searched for a bathroom. We entered an office building whose front door was unlocked although it was Saturday. We used the bathroom and on our way out a security guard grabbed my arm. I was terrified. He said I had no reason to be in the building because I didn't work there. I sputtered out that I was just using the bathroom. He said he would call the police unless I let him go through my backpack. I let him look through my backpack. Only when he was satisfied that I hadn't stolen anything did he let me go.

This incident, relatively early in my immigration to Canada, taught me an important lesson: security guards and police tended NOT to be on the side of racialized people. Instead, they saw a face that they associated with stealing and dishonesty. I began to understand that I could not trust them. My girlfriend who was walking ahead of me asked what had happened. I said, "Nothing, he was just asking me a few questions."

I visited Europe in the summer of 1972 before I attended university in the fall. It was customary in the seventies to go to Europe before university. I planned to use London, England as my base, then go to the continent and then return to London before heading back to Toronto. I loved London, England. I stayed with my first cousin Henry. He was the son of my mother's eldest sister, auntie Anne. Henry was twenty-five years older than I was. He had left Trinidad when I was three years old and had never returned. He was in the Air Force in World War II and was frustrated when he returned to Trinidad after the war and didn't find what he expected as suitable employment. He lived in London with his English wife, Pat, in a small home close to the tube.

They were excited to see me and treated me as family. I visited the British Museum, the British Library, the Tower of England, Big Ben, Buckingham Palace, Hyde Park, St. Paul's Cathedral, and Westminster Abbey. I had studied "A" level history in Trinidad, and I stared at the original copy of the Magna Carta, a document that I had studied in detail just a few years before. By far my greatest enjoyment in London was going to the theatre. I still remember some of the plays I saw. They included: Shakespeare's *King Lear*; a comedy, *There's a Girl in my Soup*; and the racy *Oh Calcutta*, plus a few more. I would often go to both a matinee and an evening show in one day.

In Europe I visited France and saw the popular sites including the Eiffel Tower, the Louvre, Notre-Dame Cathedral and I walked along the famous Champs d'Elysees. I clutched the ubiquitous *Europe on Five Dollars a Day* by Arthur Frommer, which I used as a guide to find hotels and restaurants.

I then took the train to Bern, Switzerland, to visit an old boyfriend, Peter. On the train I met two guys from Detroit, Michigan, Keith and John. I suggested they stay in Bern for a few days and see the sites with Peter and myself and they did. Peter took me to Lucerne to spend a couple days with friends I had met in Toronto. I still remember the site of the mountain, Jungfrau, covered with snow in the middle of the summer. I was then off to Cologne, Germany, with its twin cathedrals, then Amsterdam, my last stop before returning to England. Both Keith and John begged me to change my plans and travel with them for a couple days instead, but I didn't feel safe travelling with two guys I had only known for a few days, so I declined with the promise that we would get together when I returned to Toronto. I felt safer on North American soil.

Back in Toronto, I casually mentioned to my brother that I was thinking of heading to Detroit for a weekend visit with two friends that I had met in Europe. My brother insisted that I not go. He asked, "Don't you know anything about the Detroit riots?" I didn't, of course. At sixteen in Trinidad I had no knowledge of American history; the Klu Klux Klan, Jim Crow, lynching, bussing: I knew nothing. It wouldn't be until I attended the University of Guelph and studied third world politics and Black history that my eyes were opened. There was no Google for me to have a quick read on the Detroit riots, so I listened to my brother's description of what had occurred. Keith and John were white Americans. The visit was obviously a no-go.

Chapter 6

Guelph, Ontario, 1972 - 1976

I arrived in Guelph in September 1972 to begin my degree program in food science at the University of Guelph. The campus had large green spaces, so different from the two cities in Canada in which I had lived. There was also the Arboretum, with its walking trails, natural woodlands and beautiful meadows to meander through when you wanted to think quietly and have peace with nature. My first semester involved general science courses: calculus, chemistry, psychology, biology and physics. Now remember, my high school program did not have a science component. The only science course that I had completed in Trinidad at "A" levels was calculus. My first-year physics course was the most difficult; I just didn't get it, and I struggled. We had our first midterm examinations after 6 weeks. I passed all my midterms except physics. I only got 35%. I had never failed anything in my life! I phoned my brother and cried on the phone, "What am I going to do?"

I found a male friend who said he would tutor me. I was looking to regain the confidence that said, "I can achieve anything that I put my mind to." I was able to get 65% in the second midterm, so I went into my final exam with 50% overall. I passed the course at the end of the semester. I also realized, however, that I was in the wrong program. Food science would prepare me for working in a lab for a company doing basic or commercial research. I knew that I wanted to work with people; people to whom I taught nutrition. I wanted to write about nutrition. So at the end of this first term, I switched to the applied human nutrition program. I never looked back.

University life was everything I could have wished for. I thrived socially and intellectually. In these idealistic times, I actually didn't think of university as a way to get a job but instead as a means to higher learning. I told myself I would take a course in every department on campus. Over the 4 years of my applied nutrition program, I took courses in psychology, sociology, history, political science, philosophy, and anthropology, in addition to my required nutrition courses, food science, three chemistry courses, physiology, computer science, and communications. I used up all of my electives with these courses - against my nutrition advisors' advice, of course. They thought that I should take "suggested electives" like pharmacology. I didn't, and felt very well-rounded.

I also felt free. I had been so bound by getting high marks in high school and departmental examinations that were posted to England to be corrected and the results published in the newspapers for everyone to see. At university, if I didn't like a professor, I just didn't apply myself to the course in the same way. My advisor was concerned about this; my marks were all over the place, from fifty to ninety. She said that when I applied to internship that my marks would be interpreted negatively. She also thought that I should consider switching programs since my social science electives were all high marks. I explained that I loved nutrition and that I found the social sciences easy because all it came down to was writing papers in which I would discuss one point of view against the other. I was good at debating on paper. I promised that I would apply myself more to my degree courses, which I did in my last semester.

I was attractive and popular enough at University but there were significant roadblocks that I ran into with dating. When I looked at the West Indian guys on campus there wasn't much choice. There were a couple of guys whom I thought attractive but they were dating white girls. Other West Indian guys saw me as their sister or mother: "Cecily, when you cookin' me some food." With some West Indian guys from Trinidad it all came down to "class" and where I fitted in to their social hierarchy.

One incident occurred when I was hanging out with a group of West Indians. I was particularly interested in a mixed race Trinidadian named Raymond. (We would call him "red" in Trinidad but this is a description that mainly Trinidadian's understand). I spent a lot of time talking to him and then he set me straight. He said he knew of me in Trinidad. I didn't remember him. He said he was from a working-class family, and that he lived in an area four miles east of Port of Spain that I wasn't familiar with, although he had attended Queens Royal College. He recounted that at a party in Port of Spain, he had asked me to dance and I refused. He thought I had been too "stuck up" to accept a dance with him.

I know the Cecily I was back then and I probably had refused to dance with him. If I had accepted his advances and had gotten to the stage of dating him, my family would have been alarmed that I would date someone from a family they didn't know! That was in high school, of course, when Trinidad teenagers were more influenced by their parent's prejudices. Although I had changed in Canada, I was still aware of who I was. I wasn't white, so in Canadian terms, I was Black. But I still had to factor in class, or perceived class, into my assessment of others. I saw all the West Indians as a group. We were on the same side; we were university students, part of the educated elite. But I also had to think of how they saw me, with their own class prejudices. Raymond didn't see me as part of his circle, and he wanted nothing to do with me; he couldn't put behind him the girl I had been in Trinidad.

In terms of the white students, I knew that there were some whose parents wouldn't accept me, so even if they wanted to be friends, why bother? Some of the white students were first generation; born in Canada from immigrant parents, and if there was one thing I understood, it was that their parents wouldn't want their children to be friends with a West Indian immigrant. And then there was another group of white males who saw all Black women as sex objects. I didn't want anything to do with this group either. My prospects for dating were getting pretty slim. Some West Indian men eliminated me as someone they would want to date, and I had also eliminated two sets of white Canadian men.

My first boyfriend at university was Victor, in my second semester. The University of Guelph had a "steel band," a very typical Trinidadian musical instrument made out of tuned steel drums. Victor played in the steel band. He adored me and I really liked him. He was easy to talk to and we spent a lot of our spare time together. His parents were Danish immigrants who owned a farm just outside of Toronto. His eldest brother worked the farm with his parents and maintained the household. This should have alarmed me as Victor fitted into this group of first generation Canadians whose parents might have been prejudiced towards me. But when I asked Victor about this he said he was convinced that his parents would like me.

Victor's sister Carol was married to a fellow named John, and Victor and I were invited to John's mother's cottage in Muskoka. The four of us headed to the cottage. I had a great time. Muskoka was another discovery and exciting experience. We passed many small lakes on our way to the cottage. They had such pristine calm waters, the day was sunny and the water glistened with a still beauty that I had never experienced. My new country was opening up to me. Up to this point, I still thought I would return to Trinidad after graduation, but Muskoka showed me that there was so much more to discover in this vast new land.

It also reminded me of being "down the islands" in Trinidad. I water-skied for the first time in Canada and got along great with

John's mother, Ilene. She was English and I discovered she loved curry dishes, so we headed off together to find curry powder in the rural grocery store near the cottage. That evening I cooked supper for all of us. Ilene had made scones for tea, which of course reminded me of Tantie Vie's high teas and we had a good time chatting about my very Victorian great-aunt. I helped set the table and Ilene brought out some of her fine china for tea. I was able to recognize the brand. I had always been a royal watcher and tried to keep up to date with British news, so we had lots to talk about.

In the car on the drive back to Guelph, John, Carol and Victor all exclaimed that they were shocked at how well I had gotten along with Ilene, because, as they all knew, she was prejudiced against Blacks. John explained that the British were becoming increasingly concerned about the influx of West Indians, East Indians and Africans to England. I chastised them for not having told me of Ilene's prejudices and explained that I could handle myself. I said that I probably would not have acted differently because it would have been important for me to show her that her stereotypes of Blacks, were just that, stereotypes. I am still not sure if they really understood.

I was also becoming much more politically aware. In my history class, I wrote a paper on the subject of the plundering of the Caribbean by England. I tried to explain things from a political perspective to Victor, his sister and her husband; explain that the two-crop economy only benefitted the English economy; that the colonials from the third world should be able to migrate to England if they chose, and that England couldn't have it both ways. They seemed to have so little awareness of any of this and didn't engage with me at all about it. I became frustrated and dropped the subject.

My break up with Victor happened in September of 1973, after a year of dating. The main reason for this was Victor's brother and his overt racial discrimination. Victor had invited me for a weekend at his parent's farm. He came back from an earlier weekend at home, however, to tell me that he couldn't take me home for the weekend because his older brother forbade it. His older brother had actually told Victor to break up with me. He had asked Victor, "What are you thinking, dating someone Black?" It was as I had predicted. I had assessed that I wouldn't date any first generation immigrants because I assumed that they were still struggling for acceptance by the Anglo-Saxons and would perceive anyone Black as below the status they were struggling to achieve. Victor was a first generation Canadian whose parents were farmers in their home country and who came to Canada for a better life. Dating a Black West Indian immigrant was out of the question for them.

Victor was pretty shaken up. He said that he loved me. He reminded me about his desire to visit Trinidad with me at some point, about the fact that he played in a steel band with the campus steel orchestra, and that he had many close West Indian friends. Although Victor was on my side, he didn't see that this was a turning point in our relationship. I couldn't be with someone whose parents and extended family didn't accept me for who I was. I knew very well that all relationships had their ups and downs and that, when things were not going well, Victor would turn to his family for support and they would counsel him, "I told you so." I had come from a divorced family and I was adamant that I would never expose my children to a similar fate if I could help it.

My second reason for breaking up with Victor is that he came from a family where English was obviously a second language: his vocabulary and grammar were atrocious. Verb tenses, conjugations, pronouns – these were all foreign to him. I do not know how he got into university with such poor verbal and written skills. But when I thought about it, he was in engineering, not a field where grammar was necessarily important. Early in our relationship I had gently pointed out his language deficits to him. He was totally unaware of them. I asked him if I could help him with his language skills and he agreed. I would remember a few of his grammar mistakes from during the day, and in the evening I would tell him what he had said and the grammatically correct way to say them. He was making progress, but he had such a long way to go before I could take him home to Trinidad on vacation to meet my family. The "Queen's English" is very important to middle-class Trinidadians. Being able to speak well was the one sure way by which Trinidadians distinguished class.

The third reason for breaking up with Victor was the fact that I had met the man who would become my future husband, although neither of us knew that at the time. Wayne Alexander and I had met in my first semester and we had spent lots of time chatting and teasing each other. Everyone had a special cubby in the library where they studied, and Wayne's cubby was across from mine. Many times throughout an evening he could be seen hanging over my cubby chatting. He was very handsome and tall with blue eyes. He even had an Afro! His Scottish roots had given him his brown curly hair. Perhaps most importantly, however, he was also the gentlest person I knew.

He was unassuming, intelligent, good looking and unaware of any of these qualities. I had a major crush on Wayne, despite being in a relationship with Victor. Wayne of course had a girlfriend; she was completing her masters' degree in library science at the University of Western Ontario, and Wayne knew I was dating Victor. I also knew he would hitch hike to London, Ontario, on weekends when his study load permitted. One of Wayne's plans was to attend the summer semester because he planned to teach skiing over the winter semester at Snow King Ski Club in the city of Franklin.

I knew that I needed to end my relationship with Victor soon, and I knew that Wayne would be in Guelph over the summer, so I decided to attend the summer semester. Wayne was studying agriculture; none of our courses overlapped except computer science. I went to my advisor and pleaded with her to let me sign up for the summer semester and to take computer science in my third semester instead of my fifth. Although she advised against it, I did sign up that summer, taking mainly electives. The first week of classes Wayne was nowhere to be seen! Had I made my plans in vain? In the third week of the semester, I bumped into Wayne on our way to the library. I casually asked him where he'd been. He said that he had driven to Florida with his sister and a couple friends, and that they were having such a good time that they had decided to stay a couple of extra weeks.

I arranged for him to come over to my apartment for dinner to go over what he had missed in computer science. My roommate, Annemarie, asked, "So who is the special date? Is he a new boyfriend?" I said, "No, you remember Wayne, whom I study with? He is just a good friend." She shook her head in disbelief. I had skipped classes that day, baked a chicken, stuffed it, and made three side dishes. This didn't look like a casual meal. Wayne came over, and as he ate the gourmet meal I served, he said he hadn't eaten that well for a long time.

Later that evening, over a rum and coke, Wayne kissed me. I was elated. He told me that he had had a crush on me for the past two semesters but was too shy to ask me out, plus he knew I had a boyfriend. I said that I also had had a crush on him but that I knew he also had a girlfriend. This happened when I knew I could not have a permanent relationship with Victor but was still months before I made any final decisions. I continued to see Wayne during the week on campus, and Victor on weekends. This was, after all, the seventies and not particularly unusual. I even told Victor about Wayne.

The last three weeks of summer Victor and I still went on a trip we had been planning. We were going to drive from Ontario to Vancouver Island, camping. To this day I have fond memories of that remarkable trip. Driving across Canada from east to west is an incredible way to see Canada. I can still remember the shores of Lake Superior, with waves as big as the ocean, driving across the prairies into the foothills, then through the mountains on a sunny summer day in Banff. The stark beauty of it all was mesmerizing; the Okanagan Valley with its endless fruit trees, the stunning clear blue lakes and, of course, beautiful Vancouver Island, where we visited the spectacular Butchart Gardens, a site I would never forget. My heart was in love with this beautiful new country.

There was only one downside to this trip: we visited Edmonton. I still had friends there, but as we entered the city I became physically sick. I was dizzy and I had to throw up. Victor thought I had suddenly caught a bug. It wasn't a bug, however, but the many unpleasant memories that had come over me like a shroud. I was melancholy for a day or two after. It was hard to explain to Victor about my time in Edmonton, so I didn't. So much had changed in my life since then.

After our trip out west, I returned to Guelph for my fourth semester. Both Victor and Wayne were on campus and I realized I had to make a choice. I broke up with Victor our second week back. This was one of the hardest decisions I have ever had to make. Yes, I hurt Victor very much. He drove into Toronto begging my friend Deanne to talk some sense into me. She couldn't. My mind was made up. Wayne hadn't made a commitment to a relationship with me, but in spite of that I knew I couldn't continue with Victor. His family, especially his older brother, would eventually come between us.

It is surprising that the prejudice that I encountered at university and at the Snow King ski club, where Wayne worked that winter, was from Wayne's friends and roommates. They thought it funny to call me "the spook", or variations on "go fetch", treating me like a maid. "Cecily, get me a beer," or "Go get this," and "Pass me that." At the time, I didn't know how to deal with this behaviour so I just tried to ignore it.

I did try to understand why, however. I tried to understand what it was in that other person's background that made them hurtful towards me in that way. I didn't understand at this time the ingrained prejudice and stereotypes that whites in Canada had felt against Blacks for generations. Their prejudices originated, I think, from the days of slavery and those stereotypes hadn't changed. Some of their behaviour I'm sure, had to do with perceived class and status. But why would they demean me? Did it make them feel more important?

One of the guys, Bruce, was the most repetitive with the slurs and insults. I asked what his father did for a living. Apparently, he had been a laborer all his life, and moved from job to job in the small town he was from. At the time it gave me some satisfaction to know that I came from a more educated and accomplished family than he did. A couple of years after university – Wayne and I were married by this time - we got an invitation to Bruce's wedding. Wayne ended up going with another couple, but I refused to go. They tried to convince me to go and could not understand why I wouldn't. They knew how Bruce had treated me, but they just didn't understand how this was so wrong, insulting and hurtful to me.

Another significant incident that occurred at this time was at a pub in Walkerton, Ontario, close to Wayne's parents' farm. We were having some drinks with Wayne and about six other friends. No other Black person was in the pub. Actually, for years I was the only person of color in Walkerton and the surrounding towns when I went up to the farm with Wayne on the weekends. There were about eight of us, six guys and two girls, including myself. This very drunk guy stood up at the door and kept calling me a "jigaboo." That was the first time I had heard the word but I understood that it was a racial slur. This went on for a while. No one at our table, the servers or bar owners, or any other patrons in the pub said anything to this man or tried to remove him. I realize now that at some level they agreed with his slur. Later, I asked Wayne why he hadn't done something. He said, "The man was drunk, I didn't want to start a fight; I thought it was best to ignore him." I knew that a Trinidadian Black man would have beaten the guy's brains out.

Why would I stay with a man who didn't defend my honor? The answer is complicated. I knew I could only be with a white Canadian if I found him to be totally neutral to people of color or Black people. I knew that Wayne didn't have any Black prejudice himself. He grew up on a farm in Cargill, Ontario. He went to a one-room public school and then to high school in nearby Walkerton, Ontario. Everyone looked like him and the community was homogeneous. His first exposure to anyone Black or any person of color was when he left home to go to university. He loved me and everything about my culture from the food, the rum and the beauty of the Caribbean. He thought me exotic in a good way, not because of the stereotypical assumption that all Black women were hypersexual. He really loved our differences as much as our similarities. My love for Wayne was genuine; we were always so happy to see each other. We would lie side by side for hours. Just being in each other's company made us happy.

We both enjoyed the outdoors. I loved being at the farm and getting up in the early morning and going for a walk in nature, through the corn fields, when it was so quiet.

Wayne taught me to ski, a sport I had wanted to learn since my youth in Trinidad. Skiing got me outdoors in the winter. I looked forward to not only the exhilarating feeling of conquering a difficult run, but also the cold breeze on my cheeks and the trees after a night's snowfall, all covered with icicles, all white, so white and silent. Wayne wanted to travel, which was also one of my dreams. We both wanted to see the world.

Unfortunately, Wayne didn't understand prejudice and how it made someone feel. I remember saying to him once that he didn't understand any form of prejudice because he had never been called a name or had a slur thrown at him. What could anyone say about him? He wasn't short, he didn't wear glasses, he wasn't fat, he wasn't female, and he wasn't Italian, Greek or Eastern European. He was a white, Anglo-Saxon male, at the top of the pecking order. What would someone shout at him?

He tried to understand, but I realized that he couldn't experience the injustice. He couldn't feel it, really FEEL it, in his soul. For those who are the recipient of racial slurs, your self-esteem, your impressions of yourself, how you think of who you are, all these are affected. My ability to externalize these slurs has, I believe, been my saving grace. I refuse to let a slur become my reality. I always saw slurs or prejudice as something limited in the other person's character. I also thought once someone met me and really understood who I was that I would be able to change the other person's prejudice. I would realize much later how naïve that was. I was still in my twenties and still naive. I had been in Canada for just four years at this time. What I came to understand much later was that the prejudices of other people don't change much; they just saw me as an exception and still held their negative beliefs of Black people.

At the time, I thought that Wayne's lack of prejudice of people of color and Blacks was a positive characteristic. It would unfortunately prove to be a negative characteristic some years later when it came to understanding how to deal with his mixed-race children. Wayne was the least aggressive person I knew. After my experience with my father and mother I was determined to be with a non-aggressive partner, someone kind and gentle. Wayne's personality fit the bill. He was my chosen partner.

Although the prejudice was annoying and uncomfortable when it occurred, I had become a changed person. In the seventies the "Black is beautiful" movement was strong. In my first semester I went to a natural hairstyle. Not by conviction but by chance. When I arrived at Guelph from Toronto I still roller-set my hair and would spend at least an hour under the dryer, because my hair was so thick. Well, one Saturday morning at my residence, after I shampooed my hair, I went into our common area to chat with some of my roommates about the parties/bars everyone attended on Friday night. This was when my friend Debbie came into the common area and shouted, "Cecily, I love your hair, what a great curly Afro." I rushed to the bathroom and looked at my reflection. Yes my hair had dried, no roller set and there before me was my new look, a curly Afro. I loved it! It was here to stay.

I had long ago gotten over any concern about my lips or my nose. My boyfriend seemed to love my lips, and my "Hailey Mills" nose was O.K. too. Now my natural, curly afro hair completed my look. Being black was beautiful and I didn't want to be anything else. I was proud of who I was and my African roots.

This is a picture of Wayne and me. My children love this picture of both their parents with Afros. Wayne's hair was a very tight curl from his Scottish background. I used to tease him and say "I came all this way to Canada to marry a white man with kinky hair?"

In my sixth semester, I had the opportunity to research the subject of race in Trinidad in my third-world history course. My major paper was, *In the Caribbean, color is as important as economic class: an essay on racial stratification in the West Indies*. I have shared earlier that I did "A" level history in Trinidad, and was reasonably knowledgeable about British and European history, but that I really knew very little about Trinidad and West Indian history. I delved into books and articles on my chosen topic and was surprised at how much I found and how the analysis reinforced my beliefs and personal experience of race in Trinidad.

I came to understand that the racial situation in the Caribbean is very different from the racial situations in other countries that had a colonial slave history, especially the United States. One main reason, I realized, was that Trinidad's Black and colored/mixed race population was in the majority while in the United States Blacks have always been in the minority. As a result, Trinidad knew nothing about lynching or about Jim Crow. Trinidad never had segregated schools, churches, theaters, or restaurants. Even the word "colored" in the Caribbean signifies a distinct group, different than whites or Blacks, and having its own class differences as well. In the U.S., one drop of negro blood made a man a negro. In Trinidad, one is white, colored, or Black according to the color of one's skin. In the U.S. a person was classified as a negro if their negro ancestry could be found within the previous four generations. In the Caribbean one could be considered white in the second generation if your skin color was light enough.

I had many white girlfriends at University but one of my gauges of true friendship was whether or not they would "take me home to mother." This was a criteria I developed to assess the possibility of true friendship. Was your friendship true enough to show me off to your parents? One of my first visits to a friend's home was when my roommate in residence, Cathy, asked me to her home for a holiday. She lived in Owen Sound, a small city north of Guelph. Her father was a lawyer with his own practice, her mother a stay-at-home mom. She had two brothers, both at the University of Toronto, both older than Cathy and one studying law with the intention of joining his father's firm.

They lived in a lovely big home. Cathy rode horses and competed in equestrian sports before university. I loved the first visit and I think her parents really liked me, so the visits were repeated. Her mother would cook a hearty home-made meal with a delicious dessert. After dinner, I often enjoyed spending time with Cathy's parents looking at home movies of Cathy and her brothers as kids. They also owned a comfortable cottage on Georgian Bay, and I visited them there during the summer holidays. They were genuinely interested in Trinidad and my family there. One of the treats that I remember was spending the weekend at the King Edward Hotel in Toronto with Cathy. This was a peek into the life of Canadian luxury. We stayed in a special room that the family always reserved. We even had a bed that vibrated and gave massages. That was a special experience.

Another one of my off-campus roommates was Laura. Laura is still one of my closest friends today. She was the maid of honour at my wedding and is godmother to my oldest son. We got along famously from the beginning. We were both nutrition majors, but one thing that we had in common was that her parents were also divorced. She had two distinct families. The family that she first invited me home to visit was her mother and her stepfather, John. She told me that her stepfather ran a company that employed Blacks and that she had heard him use derogatory terms when he addressed them, so she didn't know how he would react to me. I thanked her for her honesty and told her I could look after myself.

They knew that I was from the Caribbean. The visit went well. What happened here and has happened to me often, is that after meeting me they saw an educated, well-spoken friend of their daughter. They were able to separate me from the stereotype of the poor immigrant, who's English and accent were not as clear as mine and who were from a less-cultured background. Again I was an exception. I am sure on Monday, John's prejudices to his Black staff were the same.

The summer after graduation I was heading to the U.S. to visit my brother and his family. My brother, Edward, and my sister-in-law, Jean, had moved to Corning, NY, and had had two children. I was going to visit to babysit my nieces for one week while Jean was in the hospital for a minor operation. I also wanted to discuss how I would finance my nutrition internship in Montreal, in order to become a practicing dietitian. Internship was a fifty-two-week program, during which I would not be able to work to pay for my living expenses.

I wrote my last exam and headed into Toronto where I dropped off a few resumes for summer jobs before I boarded a bus taking me to Corning, New York, to visit my brother's family. After he completed his MBA at Cornell University in Ithaca, New York, Edward had obtained a management position at Corning Glass Works. The bus stopped at the border and we all lined up to be interviewed by U.S. immigration. It was my turn and I was asked the usual questions of where I was going and why.

The guard asked me who my brother worked for and what did he do? I said, "My brother works for Corning Glass as a manager in accounting," and added, "I think everyone in Corning works for Corning glass." The border guard became very red around his collar and almost shouted, "I am from Corning and everybody doesn't work for Corning Glass." I only realized after the fact that he probably thought, who is this uppity Black woman with a university degree going to visit her brother whom she claims is a manager at Corning? This was the first of many negative experiences I would have in my interactions with authority figures in the United States. These were overt forms of racism. In the United States they weren't even covert, they didn't have to be, it was part of their history and how they treated all Black people.

I was refused entrance to the U.S. on the grounds that I was entering to find a job in the U.S. The border guard stamped my passport "Refused Entry." I looked at another nearby border guard who was looking at me sympathetically. I started to appeal to him but he immediately shook his head; he couldn't interfere although he could clearly see that his fellow officer was being unfair. I was dumped in a taxi and driven back to the Canadian side of the border where I waited until nightfall for the next bus back to Toronto. My brother warned me to downplay how I came across. After this incident I would follow his advice and act more humbly with American authority figures. His point was "do you want a reason to be stripped searched?" When he described this humiliating procedure, I became humbler and assumed exaggerated politeness when confronted.

At this time I still used a Trinidad and Tobago passport because I was a landed immigrant and not a Canadian citizen. I had five years left on my T&T passport before it would expire. For those five years, every time I came to the U.S. border, I would be asked, "Why were you refused entrance into the United States of America?"

Another time, I was travelling back into Canada with my boyfriend, Wayne. They told us to get out of the car so they could search it. I went through immigration just before Wayne. They went through my handbag and every receipt I had in it. I was even questioned about a receipt for a pair of boots that I had bought a year before in Canada. They found nothing of interest; then it was Wayne's turn. They asked, "What is your citizenship?" Wayne answered, "Canadian." Then they asked, "When did you become a Canadian citizen?" Wayne got a puzzled look on his face and replied, "I was born here."

We both had a good laugh in the car afterwards that they had considered him Trinidadian-by-association, in spite of his blue eyes, fair skin and obvious Caucasian features. He was with me and had a curly Afro. "How does it feel to be interrogated?" I asked. He just shrugged. We had gotten through.

Chapter 7

Montreal, Quebec, 1976 to 1977 & Toronto, Ontario, 1977-1978

I had chosen Montreal as the city in which I would do my year-long internship. I had heard so much about Montreal from other West Indians; so cosmopolitan, the diverse food, entertainment, fashion, music festivals and the joie de vivre as compared to the more conservative Anglo-Saxon Ontario. There were a lot of historical sites to visit, such as the Museum of Fine Arts and the Notre-Dame Basilica. Another place I enjoyed visiting was Jean-Talon market. I thought it would be a great experience to live in Montreal for my internship year. One other important feature was that it was surrounded by excellent ski resorts. I had taken up skiing after being taught by Wayne. I was lucky and was accepted into the Montreal Regional Dietetic Program. Somewhat naively, I thought that the Montreal French would understand me better, that they would be more sensitive and that there would be less prejudice. I had just read Maclennan's *Two Solitudes* after all. How naive I was. I was in for a surprise.

I had thought up to this point that I would prefer to know exactly where I stood with prejudiced people, not the subtle, often silent prejudice in Anglo-Saxon Ontario. Well, I changed my mind within my first month in Montreal. I was riding my bike over the

Cote de Neige from Du Fort Street, where I lived, on my way to the Jewish General Hospital where I was doing a placement. Halfway there I came to a crosswalk and I chose to ride my bike across to the other side. A trucker who was waiting for the light to change took offence to what I was doing and starting shouting, "Chris de neigre, va t' fourrer hostie" (God damn nigger, go fuck yourself!).

It took a moment for me to realize he was talking to me. I got on my bike at the end of the crosswalk and peddled away as fast as I could. It was at that moment that I realized that perhaps I preferred not knowing exactly what the other person was thinking.

Despite this type of incident, Montreal was as exciting as I had imagined it would be. I was living in a very secure apartment with a doorman and a pool. I had lived in old, substandard, student housing in Guelph and I didn't want to do the same thing in Montreal. I had recently received a portion of my inheritance money from my mother's estate and I would use some of it to pay my rent and living expenses for the year. I expected that at the end of the internship year I would be in a position to get a good, high-paying, professional job, so I could afford to spend my inheritance this way.

1976 was not the ideal time for anyone who could only speak English to be living in Montreal. Rene Levesque and the Parti Quebecois had come to power, and the French population was very proud of its language. I received a lot of probably deserved anger and indifference because I couldn't speak French. I tried, but never got past the most rudimentary language skills. I had even taken a conversational French course at Alliance Francaise in Toronto before moving to Montreal, but I just wasn't cutting it. No one seemed willing to help me along; you had to speak fluent French or you were shunned.

I experienced two types of people in Montreal. There were those that resented me because I could not speak French, and then there were those that accepted me in spite of it. I distinctly remember two experiences. The first was at my first clinical nutrition rotation at the Jewish General Hospital. This hospital was considered an English placement at that time. My first independent counseling session was to perform follow-up instructions to a pregnant woman. I spent all of the night before preparing. The dietitian who did the initial consult said the woman was bilingual and although her first language was French she spoke excellent English. I went in and greeted her in French and although I could do a diet history in French, I could not converse well enough to do a proper consultation. When I switched to English she insisted that she didn't understand English. I left and went back to my preceptor very shaken and concerned about the evaluation of my first consult. My preceptor actually consoled me and returned and finished the consultation.

The second incident happened on my return from a visit to Puerto Rico with my brother and his family for Christmas. I immediately took my pictures to a photo shop to be developed. When I returned a week later the guy at the counter told me the amount in French. He said, "Onze, quarante-huit." I misunderstood and said, "Four-eighty?" He repeated, "Onze, quarante-huit." When I still didn't get it right, he threw the package at me and said, "Eleven dollars and forty-eight cents. You are in Quebec, speak French." The point is, I knew enough about Quebec's history, and I could understand his frustration with me. I picked up my package, paid him and left. But I didn't feel very good about the interaction.

Despite a few isolated incidents like this, I loved the *esprit* of the French. My internship program had 9 other students; 6 were unilingual French, 2 were bilingual, and there was one other intern like me who was unilingual English. On Fridays, after our placements, we would all head to Old Montreal to the pubs and we would party like crazy. Often enough, we would end up dancing while standing on our chairs, singing loudly, and swaying from side to side.

At the end of my internship year, I really felt on top of the world. Although this memoir focuses on race and culture, this was not my day-to-day reality. I loved Canada, I had a wide variety of close friends, and my social life was active. Yes, most of my friends were white Canadians, but I also had a variety of West Indian friends, mainly Trinidadian ex-pats like myself, some of whom I had even known in Trinidad before I immigrated.

I had travelled to England and Europe (France, Switzerland and Germany) before university and I had plans to continue to travel when I could afford it. My brother, after completing his engineering degree at the University of Alberta, had gone to Cornell University to complete an MBA and after that he worked in upstate New York for Corning Glass. I had made many trips to visit him there. He was trying to encourage me to come to the U.S. and find a job there. Apparently, between affirmative action programs and the Equal Employment Opportunity Act, my brother thought I would almost be guaranteed to get a job quickly.

What my brother didn't understand was that I wanted to be hired on my qualifications. I didn't want any preference based on my race. I had also begun to be more aware of racial tensions in the U.S. and I didn't want any part of that. Although I knew there was prejudice in Canada, I knew it wasn't as common as it was in the U.S. I have accepted that Canadian racism is more covert, which can be more pernicious in some ways than overt racism, but in spite of this I knew I felt more comfortable in Canada.

I was confident, bright and now a professional. I believed that diversity was growing and that this would minimize racist attitudes. In 1977 all interns in Montreal were able to attend the Canadian Dietetic Association convention in Ottawa for a nominal fee. That was where I met my first West Indian dietitian, Judith Hutcheson Blake. She was from Dominica and her husband, Ken, was a dentist from St Kitts. Judith became my mentor and friend. Her stories from the 1950's on racism made me realize that I had had it so much easier.

When she was looking for housing in Toronto in the 1950's Judith and two friends secured an apartment to rent over the phone. When these three West Indian women arrived at the apartment, the landlady, seeing that they were women of color, refused to let them in, saying that they were prostitutes. In spite of the fact that this woman's complaints could not be substantiated, the three had to look for alternate accommodation. This again is an example of assigned identity that Canadians held of anyone Black. Ken, her husband, had similar challenges in securing accommodation at that time.

Both Judith and Ken were from well-to-do families in the Caribbean and when they were attending university in Halifax, Nova Scotia. Ken and six West Indian friends went to an upscale restaurant in the city. They waited to be served – and waited, and waited.... Donald, Judith's brother, asked to speak with the manager and sternly demanded to be served. The manager and staff were not accustomed to assertive, middle-class, Black customers. They were prepared to discriminate against this group because they thought they were Nova Scotian Blacks, probably from Africville, Nova Scotia, a small, poor, racialized community of predominantly Black Canadians, whose ancestors were formerly free Loyalist Blacks. There was long-standing and open discrimination in Halifax against the Black community. This group of West Indians obviously refused to be painted with the same brush. They were served immediately. My main take-away from this story is an affirmation of my attitude: expect nothing less than equal treatment.

It has been during my 40-year career as a dietitian where I have encountered the most exposure to racism, racial stereotyping, and microaggressions. This was not always on a daily basis, but it was prevalent. An important fact that should be kept in mind is that most Canadians don't think they are prejudiced. Often, I have related examples of prejudice that concerned me to my white friends, and my friends have discounted these feelings by saying things like, "That is not prejudice. They are just jealous of you; you are too bright, too well dressed, or they are intimidated by you." None of these explanations really addressed or showed an understanding of what I was feeling and experiencing. Often, it discouraged me from voicing my concerns. So I just stopped.

After internship I moved back to Toronto to find a job in my field. I was able to stay with friends, but after a month of job hunting I still had no offers. I had no direct contacts in my field but I had to find a job. So I used an old contact and was offered a municipal government job to manage a project for 6 months called the Black Outreach Project. The project involved outreach in East York, Toronto, a part of Toronto that had not been very diverse until mid-1970, when the immigration of Blacks increased significantly. In 1977 the main goal of the project was to educate relevant agencies about Blacks in their community. The strategies for achieving this goal were to visit agencies, develop learning materials, and to plan workshops for groups such as the police, social workers, other relevant government departments, and retail stores in East York.

I had four Black employees reporting to me, but we weren't alike. The main similarity was that we weren't white. We were all Black but we were from all different parts of the world. Four of us were immigrants to Canada, but there was one, third-generation Canadian, whose ancestors came to Toronto a century before and who definitely resented being asked what island she was from. There was also an African male on the project team. He said that as a Black African he didn't identify with Black Americans or West Indians because his history and heritage did not include slavery. The other two West Indians on the project team and myself were coloured/Black but we were from different islands, different classes - and different shades!

In spite of our heterogeneity, I was able to unite us sufficiently so we could focus on our main goal of putting forward a united front on educating East Yorkers on how to reach out to the Black community. Our workshop turned out to be very successful; it certainly revealed gaps in community understanding. It also opened my eyes even more to, not only the ignorance, but also the stereotypes that whites in East York had about the Blacks in their community. One of the city counselors said, "How could so many people live in one small apartment, where does everybody sleep?" She also said, "You know we get complaints about the strong smells of food in the corridors coming from those apartments."

I had a hard time understanding this kind of ignorance about basic societal facts. I wanted to tell her, "They are poor, underemployed, and are just trying to get by," and "They are simply cooking meals with different spices and other ingredients." Instead, we answered, as politely and as accurately as we could, and hoped her attendance at our workshop would put a more human face to the Blacks in her community.

One of the nice things that happened while I was working on this project was that the Toronto Star wrote an article about the changing culture of Toronto: *The Caribbean in your supermarket*. It included a picture of me shopping for typical Caribbean food in a local supermarket; looking at vegetables such as eddoes and dasheen. The article also included recipes for typical West Indian food such as stewed chicken with pigeon peas and callaloo. The article was a very positive recognition of the work I was doing on my project.

My year in Montreal had put a strain on my relationship with Wayne. We had decided to give each other some "space" until I had become more settled. During my short stay in Toronto I made friends with another Trinidadian, Ian, whom I admired. I hadn't known him in Trinidad but I believed our parents knew each other. We could talk easily and he took me to the Underground Railroad in Toronto where we would have long intellectual discussions on race, culture and West Indian immigrants in Toronto. Ian was a social worker. He would be called in to defuse racial tensions that arose in schools. I found this occupation fascinating and I asked him how I might have dealt with incidents such as the ones I had experienced at the University of Guelph. I told him that I normally just dealt with it by ignoring the derogatory comments. Ian said that was not the best way to handle it. He shared an alternative way of handling those situations.

He suggested that if someone white came out with a racial slur to an ethnic person, the ethnic person should say, "I find that offensive," and then to use some "I" messages such as, "I feel hurt/upset/sad/ when you say that to me."

Armed with this simple approach, I used it often on anyone who said anything to me or to a crowd that I found offensive. Later on, this included some of the same people who had used racial slurs at me before. Wayne's old friends who worked at Snow King Ski Club – the one who had called me names - might start with a Newfie joke, or a Chinese joke - it didn't have to be about Blacks - and I would say, "Guys, that joke is offensive to me." In the bar, many a time, someone would start to tell a joke or make a comment and then they would look at me and stop in their tracks because they knew how I would respond. I am not so naïve to think that I stopped their racial biases, but I do know that I didn't have to listen to them, and around me at least it made them pause.

At that time I began to delve into the available resources that were intended to help immigrants deal with ethnic and racial discrimination. This was, after all, the time when Toronto in particular, but also many other parts of Canada, began to see large numbers of immigrants from non-white communities settling in Canada. My research helped me develop better understanding about race relations. It affirmed many of my assessments and genuine feelings, and as well gave me ways to deal with the kinds of intolerance I had encountered.

There were some important takeaways for me at this time, such as the fact that everyone here, except the indigenous peoples, is or was an immigrant since they or their ancestors all immigrated to Canada at one time; another takeaway was that some people who immigrate to Canada from traditional source countries (the U.S., and western or northern Europe) were accepted almost immediately as Canadians. What distinguished those who were looked down on as immigrants from those who were accepted almost immediately as Canadians? Skin color is often very important. The accent, language or religion of the newcomer may affect how quickly he or she is accepted. Immigrants who are not accepted quickly may have to work at low-paying jobs because better jobs are not available to them.

There are important ways in which immigrants and non-immigrants are the same. They are both workers, the producers of everything real in this country. They build and run the mines, farms, factories and railways. They all want a better life. Unlike their employers, they don't own very much. And I learned some of the arguments and comments that racially intolerant people are likely to make: "You come here to have it easy! They just let you in, no problems! You're lazy and you don't fit in! You cause racism, crime and overcrowding! You live off welfare! On top of all that you take away jobs and hurt the economy. Why don't you go back where you came from!"

Between 1900 and 1930 nearly two-thirds of all immigrants were from traditional source countries, like Great Britain, France and the United States. After the war, more immigrants came from white, eastern European countries that were dealing with large numbers of refugees. Beginning in the 1970's, more and more immigrants came from non-white countries, often former colonies and countries that had a slave history; many of these were economic and political refugees. In the years leading up to WWI, Blacks from the U.S. were actively being discouraged from immigrating to Canada by Canadian agents in the U.S. At the same time, Canada made a "gentleman's agreement" with the Japanese government limiting Japanese immigration to Canada to 150 per year.

A common complaint against immigrants is that they don't try to become Canadian. This doesn't take into consideration immigrants' contribution to Canadian culture. Many immigrants come from old and well-established cultures and are very proud of their traditions. Immigrants vastly enrich Canadian culture. Even while they want to keep some of their old traditions, most want to become a part of Canadian life, especially in succeeding generations.

Discrimination is not always based on color. There have always been certain immigrant groups who are made scapegoats. First it was the Irish, then it was the Chinese. Later on it was the East Europeans and the Italians. It is usually the latest group to arrive - the most vulnerable group, and the least understood – that gets all the blame. This last takeaway helped me understand how accurate some of my earlier assessments had been, first in Trinidad, then in Edmonton and most recently in Toronto, such as when I experienced the blatant prejudice by an Italian mother and then by an Eastern European mother. They were the last groups to arrive and wouldn't associate with a group perceived to be lower than them.

Chapter 8

Madison, Ontario, 1978-1979: Hopewell Hospital First Job, Marriage

I got my first job as a clinical dietitian at a Hopewell hospital in Madison, Ontario. One of my Toronto friends asked me, "Why Madison?" since it was known as one of the more conservative municipalities in Canada, certainly not very diverse. I said it was because I wanted to finally start my career in dietetics and that the first place to hire me as a clinical dietitian was Madison, so that was where I would go.

The hospital had three positions advertised. I was hired to complete a six month maternity leave, not a permanent position. In spite of that I felt very confident and moved into an apartment. This job was everything I could want in my first professional position. I was in outpatient counseling and I was very keen to prove that I could excel. I applied myself, developed pamphlets, and was committed to all my patients with whom I went above and beyond to meet their needs. I was able to form a positive relationship with my two managers Eleanor and Mila. I was fortunate, then, when another dietitian left her job at the same time as my six-month maternity leave position was finishing and I was hired into a full-time position.

Wayne and I reunited when I moved. We became engaged at Christmas, 1978, and were married on May 19th, 1979. Wayne and I had been dating since 1973. Before and after we married we had a large social circle. It came about that we would divide our friends by season because that was when we could socialize with them. In the winter we spent our time with our ski friends. Wayne was a snow school instructor (ski and snowboarding), starting out as assistant director and then becoming director after we were married.

In the winter, Wayne worked as a snow school instructor at the Snow King ski club outside of Franklin, Ontario. In the summer, he farmed his 75 acres on weekends with his father in Cargill, Ontario. In order to earn some money in the summer months, Wayne began to manage a pool company that belonged to a friend in a small town just outside of Franklin. In spite of this, I was still the only one with a full-time job that included employee benefits. Wayne and I had decided quite a while before that we would settle in the city where one of us had a full time job. That should have meant that Wayne would move to Madison, where I was working, but instead, Wayne convinced me to look for a full-time job in Franklin.

To anyone who questioned me about our living apart, I would remind them that Wayne and I had been together for six years, and that I would move to Franklin after I got a professional job offer there. I preferred the challenges of working in a teaching hospital, so I set about looking at job possibilities at Restora Care in Franklin and not a smaller general hospital.

I set up an interview with Restora Care in Franklin but was not offered a job. I had a very supportive manager, Eleanor, in my job in Madison. She even phoned the manager in Franklin to personally ask her to consider me for employment. Eleanor told her counterpart about my dedication to my patients and that I often went above and beyond.

As Eleanor related to me later, the Restora Care manager, Margaret, told her that she thought I was "too outspoken" when she interviewed me and described a variety of other personality traits that she didn't like. It all seemed so subjective and didn't appear to have anything to do with my work ethic, competence and job performance. She had met me for just half an hour a month earlier. Were these assumptions based on the stereotypes of Blacks that I had heard before? I realized while doing my research for this book that the Restora Care manager continued to have many Black stereotypes that she unjustifiably assigned to me. Thankfully Eleanor was able to convince the manager that I was none of the things that she had described to her, and that she should give me a second chance.

Eleanor also told her that I was newly married and living apart from my husband who worked in Franklin. I was granted a second interview, and, with Eleanor's coaching, I cut my enthusiasm in half and was as docile as I could be. I got the job.

Chapter 9

Franklin, Ontario, 1979-1986: Restora Care, Children

I worked at the Restora Care hospital for seven years. I loved my role and worked at being a progressive practitioner. I gained the respect of the doctors I worked for. The early 1980's were still the early days of nutrition support in hospitals, but I was able to bring my practice to the point of being able to write orders and to develop tube feeding and nutritional assessment protocols. I even organized one of the first nutrition support workshops at our hospital in 1981, with other dietitians, physicians and pharmacists. This was fairly progressive at this time. I also had my sights set on eventually moving into management, so I began taking part-time business courses at a university within driving distance as a start towards getting my MBA.

It was in Franklin where Wayne and I had many firsts. We bought our first home and two of our sons were born at Restora Care where I worked. I should share that my first pregnancy resulted in a miscarriage. Of course, my thoughts went back to my abortion in Trinidad more than ten years before. It stirred up my greatest fears that I had damaged my reproductive system and I wouldn't be able to have children, one of my deep maternal desires. I dreamed of having a family. Wayne and I were now settled with our own home, I was successfully working in a full time job, and we were ready. With a lot of prayers I became pregnant again, and in August 1982 I was rewarded with my beautiful first son, Davin Alexander. I chose his name carefully. The meaning of his name is "beloved," and he was.

The celebrations were big and joyful. We had a big christening party where our friends and family came from all over Ontario. My brother and his family all came up from the U.S. I loved this little new addition to our family. Wayne would return home after work and ask if he had moved from lying on my tummy where he slept all day, the answer was no. Just twenty-three months later his brother, Ryan, was born, my second son, another perfect healthy baby, and our family seemed complete. He was the baby, or youngest child for six years. Little did we know at this time that down the road there would be a third addition.

My middle son's fourth birthday party with his cousins at Wayne's parents' farm. My older son is seated next to his brother

It is interesting how at an early age little personalities are formed. My sons were very different in personality. My oldest seemed more cautious and conscientious, like many first-borns, while my second son was more free-thinking and independent; he always seemed to be getting into little mischievous "fixes." His main characteristic was his imagination. By three he had created a world of "miniatures." He was the only one who could see them. He would tell me elaborate stories of their adventures. I wish I had kept a diary of these stories. I would rush home after work to be with them. My life had a new purpose. Before my two sons, I had thought of returning to university full time but now realized that this goal was in the future, since I now had two precious lives to concentrate on.

Working as a snow school director was Wayne's winter occupation for all of our married life. So we spent our winters skiing. We would go on ski vacations together and, after we had kids, we would go on March break ski vacations as a family. Wayne loved to ski. He had two occupations: in the summer, he loved farming, and in the winter he would ski. I would joke with him that I was the real breadwinner in the family. The point is Wayne was happy doing what he loved and when he was happy, that made me happy.

I have always said that I enjoyed being part of a helping profession. Counseling as a dietitian made me feel fulfilled just knowing that I at least made one person's life better each day.

Skiing is a very social sport. Many evenings after classes I could find Wayne in the pub with other instructors, students, and friends. He insisted that this was all part of the job of a ski instructor. I really didn't mind. I spent most of my weekday evenings completing one work-related project or another at home. There was always another nutrition research article to read. I had come to understand that nutrition was one of the most dynamic professions for research and change. You always had to be on top of some new diet, drug or procedure.

Wayne and I would get together with our University of Guelph alumni couples yearly. We arranged to have reunions every five years, and sometimes in between. Typically, we would head to a Canadian resort and spend most of our time catching up and reminiscing about the good old days.

In the summers, we would spend most of our social time with Wayne's friends from his childhood at the farm in nearby Cargill and Walkerton, Ontario, where he grew up. Most of his buddies still farmed, and Wayne had purchased a seventy-five acre lot that he farmed every weekend. We would head to Cargill most weekends and spend Friday and Saturday nights socializing.

Life in the country was so different from the city. Neighbours would stop by to chat and drop off a pie they had baked or share extra vegetables they had picked that day. It reminded me of life in Trinidad. I knew that I couldn't return to live in a big city like Toronto or Edmonton where no one knew their next door neighbours in their apartments, and life was so much more impersonal. In our calendar there were local events we looked forward to every year like "Chicken Fest," which had carnival rides and local food. At Chicken Fest, we both liked to have a sausage on a bun with lots of fried onions as soon as we arrived. Local dances were another highlight where we would see even more distant friends of Wayne; some even from his high school days.

After the dances, we would often drive for a campfire at a friend's farm along the river. It was customary to camp overnight, a popular Canadian past-time. Unfortunately, I just didn't like camping, consisting as it did of sleeping on the hard ground, in an uncomfortable sleeping bag. I did camp for a few years, but then realized I could drive back to the farm and sleep in a comfortable bed, get up in the morning, have a shower, and then head back to the camp site. I would arrive fresh and awake and see the early morning risers, often slightly hung-over, and knew that I had made the right choice for me.

When Wayne was out farming with his dad, I spent a lot of time indoors with his mother. She had multiple sclerosis and was in a wheelchair. I admired her strong will as she prepared the large family meals with my assistance. What I loved best was chatting with her about what Wayne was like as a boy. He was actually very shy growing up. She told me that when he wanted to join the boy scouts, it took him three trips to actually go into the room where the meetings were held. What made Wayne more special to me was how much he loved his parents; they weren't as demonstrative as we were in Trinidad but they showed love with simple gestures and kindness. I knew in my heart I wouldn't have been his mother's choice of a wife for her son but I was thankful for his parents' acceptance of me as the partner their son had chosen.

Although they showed no prejudice to me directly, I was curious to observe if there were any prejudices in this white community that seemed so conservative and homogeneous. It was after a few years of dating Wayne that his mother asked the new name of a recent grandchild and was told that her name was "Mary Theresa." Mother looked to the ceiling and all she said was, "How Catholic." It was at that time that I began to observe and understand how this very conservative farm community was divided along religious lines, Catholic and Protestant, and there wasn't much mixing between the two. In later years I met a nurse who was from Walkerton, near Wayne's farm, her brothers were Wayne's age. I rushed home to ask him if he knew her. He listened to the name and said no, because they were a Catholic family.

A friend from the Maritimes shared with me that her small town was generally divided as the West End and the East End. The West End was predominantly Catholic, and the East End was predominantly Protestant. For a few generations, the folks in the East End had absolute disdain for the West End, based purely on religion. My friend was backpacking through Europe when she received what would be otherwise happy news that her sister had become engaged. Her great aunt, however, was horrified that her mother would "permit" her sister to be engaged to a West End Catholic. My friend was able to point out over a phone call to her mother that she was divorced from a Protestant, while her sister's fiancé was a great match for her sister. Her sister recently celebrated her 35 thirty-fifth wedding anniversary. Although this story shows that religious divides can be overcome, I am not so naïve to think that if three Black farmers had bought farms in my husband's farming community that racist attitudes would not have surfaced.

Wayne and I had an atypical financial arrangement for a married couple, but it worked for us. We split most of our joint expenses but we had separate accounts. I think this was instilled in me by my mother, to be always financially independent. Having separate bank accounts also worked for us because of our different approaches to money. I was a saver and Wayne wasn't. Yes, I spent a lot of my money on clothes and jewelry, but I refused to spend money on something I couldn't pay for in full. I was debt averse; unless it was our mortgage, I didn't want to borrow money.

We never had a car loan. For himself, Wayne would buy a cheap, used car for which we would pay cash. Even when I bought my first new van, I paid cash for it. Wayne, on the other hand, was comfortable with debt. This was perhaps because of his farm upbringing; his father was always taking out loans for expensive farm machinery, livestock, seeds, crop inputs and upkeep. They were "cash-poor and land-rich." Between farm machinery, tile drainage or some other major expenditure, Wayne always owed something to the bank. In all our years of marriage, I do not think there was ever a year that the farm actually showed a profit. At the beginning I resented this. But Wayne looked forward to farming each weekend so much, he didn't think of it as work. I changed my thinking around it. I accepted it as a potential liability but that this was his hobby. Just as some husbands spend money on golf, Wayne spent his on his hobby: farming. When he was under and needed more cash, I would transfer the money he needed; we always had enough. We had paid off the mortgage of our house after my brother and I had sold our joint property in Tobago in 1988. I suggested to Wayne that we buy a bigger house since the family would be getting larger, and so we would have to start saving towards another mortgage.

Many would say that Wayne and I were a bit unique in our marriage. One thing that made our marriage strong was that we respected each other's individuality and trusted each other to be able to do the things each of us wanted, all while being able to come together to enjoy each other's company. We understood that a successful marriage was not a matter of luck but accomplished through much understanding, a lot of accepting and trust, a lot of overlooking and a whole lot of loving.

Wayne and I didn't argue often. We joked that our only disagreements were about raising our sons. With our older boys we were more laissez-faire. With our last we established more limits and I talked to him more about values. He went to church with me and was the only son to be confirmed, although all three sons were baptized. Together, Wayne and I were in sync. We had one of our vacations together every year, just the two of us, no kids. We both looked forward to this time to reconnect with each other and be soulmates again. Our friends often commented on how we were so demonstrative with each other. After so many years together, we still interacted the same as when we had met, many years before.

Although Wayne and I did so much together with our friends and each other, it was important for each of us to have our own groups of friends that we did things with individually. I have a large group of girlfriends that I socialize with. I would say almost all are white Canadians. Did I talk race or prejudice? No, the topic hardly ever came up. Even if there was an incident that I encountered because of my race, I rarely discussed it with my white girlfriends. I did not think they would understand. This illustrates the two parts of my "parallel worlds."

For example, I have mentioned that skiing is how I spend my winters. Skiing is a sport in which many of the participants are wealthy. It is an expensive sport. Ski equipment and gear, lift passes, transportation; it all adds up. Every year, a group of my friends attended a private club in Collingwood, Ontario, for Ladies Day every year. This was usually a wild time. We would ski all day and end with a big party; lots of good food, drinking, skits and prize awards. Every year the planning group would have a theme. At one of the events the theme had the place lined with cardboard props of film stars. Two of the girls in our group decided to steal three of the props. The organizing group needed them back as they were rented. When our group found this out, our two friends returned the props to the group organizers for that year.

The following year there was another group of organizers at the ski club for Ladies Day and another theme. At skit time a group of us were standing on chairs trying to get a good view of the stage, but our view was obstructed by three big baskets of spider plants. Two girls in our group, lifted the three plants down and rested them on the floor below us. Much later that evening I had to go to the washroom. When I exited there was a girl from the organizing group who had followed me to the bathroom and was waiting to talk to me. She pulled me aside and said, "You know you can't take those plants home." I was unsure what she was talking about and then I realized that it was the plants that two girls in our group had lifted down so they could see the stage. Her assumption had been to approach the only person of color to inform her that she couldn't take (steal) these spider plants. This left me shaken.

I am not sure how I made it back upstairs. One of our friends asked me if I wasn't feeling well. The hurt was showing on my face. I knew it would not be an easy thing to explain. They would take her side and say it was just a misunderstanding. I have heard the excuses before. Parallel worlds.

In spite of my job performance and my business management courses, I was not hired for either of two, more senior positions that became available while I worked at Restora Care. The first was in our neonatal unit and involved assessing failure-to-thrive babies who were on total parenteral nutrition and enteral feeds. The dietitian who had worked in the unit had left suddenly so there was no opportunity to train a replacement. I stepped forward when no one else wanted to, did the necessary research, and trained myself on how to calculate these difficult neonatal assessments. I acted as the neonatal dietitian for six months.

At that time, another dietitian wanted to change her specialty to the neonatal unit and our manager, Margaret, removed me from the position and returned me to my previous specialty. I was devastated. When I asked for an explanation, she said I wasn't "well suited" for the position. "Well suited" sounded very subjective to me. I had received very positive feedback from the unit nurses and doctors, but my manager didn't ask for their perspective. The decision was entirely hers.

The next position to become available was the coordinator of the internship program. I thought I was a good internal candidate; I had already taken some of my pre-MBA courses and I had covered the coordinator position for the clinical area for a six-month maternity leave a year ago. In spite of this, my manager passed me over a second time. Again, she described some personality traits that she didn't think were suited for management, instead of evaluating concrete achievements and the positive relationship I had built with my staff a year before. I had written new protocols, improved communication with the aides and the diet technicians, in addition to developing many policies and procedures for the area. Despite this, she didn't hire me for this position either.

My manager, Margaret, had not had any intention of hiring me in the first place. I was only hired because my previous manager in Madison had phoned and convinced her to hire me. The same stereotypes were blocking me now from being promoted. It would not matter what I did. I had planned workshops, gained the trust of the physicians I worked with, taken MBA courses, none of these accomplishments made a difference.

At that time the hospital had a well-known chaplain, Peter, with whom I had built a good rapport. When I think back, my talks with him were often more like counseling and guidance sessions. I confided in him my frustration with my manager Margaret and asked him for advice on how I could gain her trust. The chaplain said he didn't think I would ever gain her trust. He related it to race and said that she stereotyped Blacks. I was shocked. I had always believed that hard work, more education, and going above and beyond would be my answer to getting ahead. At this stage of my professional life I thought race issues were behind me. Critical race theory would explain that Black women are stereotyped as aggressive, loud, rude and pushy.

In my six-month maternity relief position, my manager and I did the orientation to new Restora care staff where we introduced them to Nutrition and Food Services. My manager would finish her presentation and then proceed to do my presentation also. The third time we were scheduled to do the presentation, she was held back and I started before her. I could see the shock on her face when she arrived late and was able to observe how articulate I was, how I answered questions and the humour I added to the presentation. After she praised me for a job well done, I silently wondered how she thought I performed my other professional duties, the ones that involved communication, teamwork and counselling.

The chaplain, Peter, socialized with my manager and her husband and he shared some generalizations my manager had made about Blacks in general and about me in particular. And it was not only Blacks; she held similar stereotypes about Filipinos. In fact, she had had a Filipino dietitian at the psychiatric hospital fired for being "too docile." The chaplain advised me that if I wanted to advance in my profession that I should seek a management job elsewhere. I took his advice. A few months later a clinical manager's job came open at Ultra Care in Greenville, Ontario. I applied and was hired for the job. So my husband and I were moving again.

Chapter 10

Greenville, Ontario, 1986-1995: Ultra Care Hospital

The move to Greenville was stressful and challenging. It was the late-80's, a time when women thought they could do it all: have a full time, demanding job, have a family, and run a household - all at the same time. It was a time when husbands were beginning to do more around the house but it was still far from equal. I discussed with Wayne that I wanted to apply to a management position at Ultra Care in Greenville as the coordinator of clinical nutrition, and that to do this we would have to move again.

After I had given up my previous job in Madison, seven years earlier, to move to Franklin, where Wayne worked, we had decided that the next move would be mine. Wayne agreed with me applying for the job but I realized that when I got the job he really didn't think about what that move entailed. He would have to leave both the Snow King ski club and the pool company he worked for. When he finally thought this through, he didn't think he could leave them in the lurch. He suggested that I could move with the kids, and he would follow me a year later, He would come to be with us on weekends and during the week when he could. I must have been crazy, but I agreed. We sold our house in Franklin and bought a new house in Greenville. I then moved with my two sons who were one and three at the time to Greenville, Ontario.

My first crisis happened within a month of moving: I lost the nanny I had I hired. I had interviewed and chosen a nanny who would come to my home with her son who was two. The problem was that after just a month, her husband was laid off at his job at the local automotive plant and she had to return to her hairdressing job to be the breadwinner of the family. I went to the list of the applicants that I had interviewed for nanny. They all now had jobs, except one. I was desperate, however, so against my better judgment I hired her.

After a month my neighbour related to me that she thought my nanny was "out of control." My neighbour told me that she had overheard the nanny shouting and using inappropriate four letter words with the boys. I had to let her go. A good friend of mine from Trinidad, Gail Lynn, who lived at the bottom of my street, said she would take them temporarily until I found my third nanny. Gail Lynn was the one who found a great nanny for me, Brenda, a recently retired schoolteacher. She sounded perfect and I hired her on the spot. Unfortunately, she was only with me a month when her daughter, who had just returned from a vacation in Mexico, had acquired an illness that was affecting her kidneys. She was hospitalized and on dialysis. Brenda was torn between her commitments to me and her daughter who was near death's door. Her priority of course was with her daughter.

She came in on a Wednesday to say that she couldn't finish the week. I had arranged to have a couple of dietitian colleagues over that evening when I got the news from Brenda. Wayne also arrived from Franklin at the same time. I excused myself and went to the bathroom and just sobbed. What had I gotten myself into? I had to survive, I had to make things work. I had sold my house and bought a new one. I had moved my family, and taken on a new job. I had to pull myself together, I had to be strong.

At times like these I always called on my mother for strength. She had gone through similar challenges, if not greater. Yes, this was a big hurdle, but I would master it. One of the techniques I used, before I even knew it was a therapeutic technique, was "positive self-talk." I told myself that I was going to succeed, that I would be able to get over this hurdle, that I could see the finish line. I dried my eyes and put on my glasses and hoped that no one would recognize that I had been crying. I told my colleagues that I had to solve the problem of finding a nanny. I went back to my file.

When I had put the first advertisement in the newspapers looking for a nanny, a woman named Helen had called me both times. The problem with her was I had to take the kids to her place, as she ran a nursery. She could not come to my place. I phoned her that evening, told her my predicament, and she said I could come over right away to see her. I took my older son with me and headed to Helen's. The interview went well and she said I could bring both the boys over the following morning. She proved to be a great daycare person and she looked after my two sons until they started school.

My new job, on the other hand, was turning out to be exactly what I needed to grow. I had an excellent vice-president, Dennis, to whom I reported directly, and who believed in my ability to lead and restructure the clinical nutrition department effectively. He saw me as intelligent and articulate and gave me his trust. In spite of my stresses at home, I was devoted 100% to this position and worked there from 1986 to 1995, nine years. It was a welcome change from Restora Care. I had a director who had the confidence to give me the autonomy I needed to build the department of clinical nutrition. Because this was a newly created department, I started with strategic planning: Mission, Vision Statement, SWOT (Strengths, Weaknesses, Opportunities and Threats) analysis, short and long term goals, and then we developed goals and objectives for each dietitian. The list was extensive and very ambitious.

We were able to increase the number of dietitians and even encourage pure research in addition to practice-based research in all specialties. It was important to have a positive rapport with upper management, and I did. I was able to drop into the offices of the CEO, my VP, and the VP of nursing, as well as the offices of other directors and managers in areas with connections to clinical nutrition. In addition to research, clinical nutrition had an emphasis on the development of educational materials for patients, and they also encouraged entrepreneurial initiatives.

The dietitians brainstormed on entrepreneurial ideas and our most successful venture was obtaining funds from our involvement in research. Physicians would often approach dietitians for assistance after they had completed some aspects of their research projects. Many of the dietitians, in order to maintain a good relationship with the physicians, would complete physician requests on their own time. Dietitians alerted me that we could approach physicians before their research proposals were submitted to accurately calculate the dietitian hours needed, and to add an administrative fee to cover my time. The money we raised from this and other initiatives resulted in thousands of dollars in extra funds for the department.

As a result, clinical nutrition was able to contribute to the purchase of a metabolic cart for the ICU. Also, clinical dietitians were able to attend conferences in their specialties. My whole focus was to facilitate the growth of my team. This is how I defined my role as their coordinator and subsequently their manager. If they were strong and successful it would reflect well on our department and indirectly on my management. I had had a manager in the past who took the credit for projects her dietitians had completed, and I was determined not to do that because I knew how unfair that felt. The late-1980's were an exciting time to work in nutrition management and health care. Growth and adding value were emphasized. The hospital's mission was "exemplary patient care," and we did our best by going above and beyond, to contribute to the mission.

At this time we had a new addition to our happy family. I had been at Ultra Care for four years and was nicely settled in. Wayne had moved to Greenville and had been working as the snow school director at The Slopes, a ski club nearby. He still farmed in the summer and supplemented farming on weekends by working at his own pool company in the summer. Our two sons were five and seven and were at public school full time. We were comfortable financially; we had both paid off the remainder of our student loans, and we had paid off our mortgage with the last of my inheritance from Trinidad. We were debt-free!

A third child? Because of both of our ages, I decided that we should reconsider if our family was complete. We could financially afford another child and I was excited to try for a daughter this time. Wayne was not as enthusiastic as I was. He wasn't a baby dad; he was enjoying the boys at five and seven; they were now skiing and becoming involved with sports that he loved, like soccer. My friends questioned my sanity and asked why I would consider getting back into diapers, nannies and all the things that tied you down with a new baby. But I had maternal reasons and I was convinced we had enough love and means to welcome a new addition. I also thought that in terms of timing it was now or never. Wayne eventually became committed and in 1990 we welcomed our third, adorable son, Keegan into our family.

The odds were never in my favor for a girl, I guess. I knew I was having a son early in my pregnancy, and he was loved and precious from the beginning. His brothers rushed home after school to be with him. They were involved brothers at six and eight. They had even attended classes at another local hospital so that they could be present at his birth. They changed diapers and participated in all aspects of his care. This was a happy, positive time at home; little could I have predicted what lay ahead for me at work.

It was also during this period that I became a Canadian citizen. I had been a landed immigrant in Canada for twenty-two years before I became a Canadian citizen. I could have applied seventeen years before but I hadn't. It had nothing to do with how I felt about Canada, but how I perceived Canadians felt about me. I applied in 1991. This was the year when Trinidad and Tobago began to grant dual citizenship. I didn't want to give up my Trinidad citizenship altogether to become Canadian. I wanted dual citizenship. If I wasn't thought of as being Canadian, if the best I could be was a West Indian-Canadian, then I wanted dual citizenship.

By this time, I was so tired of being asked, "Where are you from? Where were you born? You speak good English, what language did you speak in Trinidad? Even if I answered I am from Greenville, Ontario the next question would be, "But where were you from before Greenville, where are you really from?" I did not mind people who were really interested in Trinidad, my first home, or their curiosity about my family and culture. But many people just stopped the questioning when I said Trinidad. I was Canadian too. I wanted to be seen as Canadian.

I had embraced the beauty and personality of being Canadian: the country, the mountains, the many lakes, the different seasons, the people. I knew I couldn't live in Trinidad again. I was Canadian, this was my home. This was my country. There were some Canadians who didn't see me as Canadian but there were many others who had accepted me and loved me for who I was. My husband and children were truly Canadian. There is a distinct Canadian personality. The personality as I saw it was how polite we were, and how often we were apologetic but proud of how great our country was, and that we were not boastful of our many achievements; how we had the habit of saying "sorry" for our greatness. This was also how I behaved and thought. After over twenty years, this was now part of my personality.

I did love opportunities to express my Trinidadian culture in Canada, however, and no better place to do this than taking part in the Caribbean Carnival parade (formerly known as "Caribana") in Toronto every year. Just "wining" (a suggestive form of dancing in Trinidad) down Lakeshore Boulevard, dressed up in bold, colorful costumes, I could express myself and be free. This was also an opportunity to introduce my Canadian white girlfriends to some of my culture.

Author and friends at Caribana

It was in the early 1990's when health care restructuring came onto the provincial agenda, and things began to change in health care. The literature was full of articles about hospital restructuring and about how health care should be delivered. The literature talked about more of a focus on direct patient care and moving to self-directed work teams, which of course decreased the need for management positions so that more funds could be assigned to patient care. These were all very admirable goals but the underlying reason for restructuring wasn't only compassion for patient care: it was the need to save dollars and make significant cuts to hospital budgets so that deficits could be reduced. The Ontario government was going to cut the money they allocated to hospitals.

A big question was: could self-directed, patient care work teams succeed when the focus was really budget savings? In 1994, after eight years at the hospital, we were told that in order to balance the hospital budgets, we were restructuring. As part of this, all mangers had to reapply for a reduced number of positions. Seventeen portfolios were created from over forty departmental management positions. The clinical portfolios were based on medical specialty teams, not on professional departments. The nephrology team, for instance, would include all the nephrologists, a manager, the floor nurses, and one each of the allied health professionals: a dietitian, a pharmacist, an occupational therapist, a physiotherapist, a psychologist, a social worker, and a speech pathologist. The professional managers, all except nursing managers, were very threatened. For me, as the manager of the clinical nutrition department, there was no medical specialty team that I could fit into. I could apply for the food service management position, but this was a non-clinical role, so I wasn't too enthusiastic about it.

It was at this time that I was approached by my director, Dennis, to see if he could be of assistance in my going back to university. I had been paying into a five-year self-directed leave plan for three years now. This meant that I was working full-time but only being paid 4/5 of my salary. Having paid into this leave plan for three years, in two more years I could take a year's leave with pay. I had intended, with this year off, to obtain my master's degree. I knew that if I didn't make the cut in this round of restructuring and downsizing, I would receive a severance package in addition to what I would be getting back from my self-funded leave. So I declined taking an early leave and instead, applied for the nutrition and food service management position.

In looking at my chances, I thought that the successful applicant for this position would be either: the present manager, an external food service contractor, or me. I had my interview. The vice president of this portfolio, Julian, not Dennis, the vice president to whom I had previously reported, invited me to his office to hear the results of the interviews for this position. I found out that none of my assumptions were correct. He had chosen a nurse, Jane, to be the manager. He had, however, saved a position for me as the coordinator of clinical nutrition and business development. I would do business development half time. In the other half I would continue to play a leadership role with the dietitians. I responded positively to the offer. He gave me the rest of the day off. The next day at work I phoned my new manager Jane, to congratulate her. We set up a meeting for 10:30 a.m. in my office.

Before I describe the next year with my new manager, Jane, in 1994-5, I need to say that she was, unequivocally, my nemesis. And in spite of my knowing this and doing everything in my power to get along with her, this year was one the most stressful and difficult years of my life. I sometimes reflect that I would have been better off if I had lost my job with the other clinical managers. But I didn't. My mentors, the two vice presidents, Dennis and Julian, who were part of the selection committee saw my worth and recognized my contributions and had designed a job for me. I had the support of my vice presidents because I excelled at my job: my work performance was my strength. Little did they know how that would work out. I do tend to be a positive person by nature and I think the experience I had demonstrated the adage: what doesn't kill you makes you stronger.

I should elaborate on why my new manager Jane was my nemesis. Prior to restructuring, when I was still in a management position, I had no line relationship with her. Jane was the director of quality assurance (QA) at the hospital, a position with no line reports. When I started at the hospital, I knew who she was and would greet her in the halls with a polite good morning or good afternoon. She would not acknowledge my good wishes and instead would glare at me as if I didn't belong there and not acknowledge my presence. This odd behaviour bothered me and, because I have always been intuitive to the behaviour of others, I sensed a strong dislike. I had discussed this with my manager as early as 1987, my first year at the hospital. I had wanted to approach the director of QA but my manager at the time, with whom I discussed this dilemma, had asked me, "What would you say to her? That she ignores you in the halls?" Realizing she was right, I buried my concerns. This was the first subtle microaggression by the woman who would become my new manager.

Shortly after I had started at the hospital, however, I did have to set up an appointment with the QA director to update her on my clinical nutrition quality assurance program. My phone calls to her office were ignored. A week later my manager said that the QA director had called her to arrange meetings with both of us to discuss the clinical QA program. My manager was a food service specialist and therefore was not familiar with the intricacies of the clinical program, so it was curious to me that the director of QA would want both of us present.

At the meetings, the director of QA, Jane, refused to speak to me directly. Instead, she directed all her questions to me through my manager, Anne. Odd you might say? It was exactly that. Just a year before, the director of QA had met one-on-one with the senior clinical dietitian, Claire, to discuss our quality assurance program at that time. Why were things so different now? I see now that her treatment of me was a complete invalidation of who I was as a person; she made me feel invisible. It was wrong, but in 1988 how could I object and what could I say? I just moved on, thankful that these were my only encounters with her and knowing that since there were no line relationships between us she couldn't hurt me.

But now she was my new boss! How would I survive? This was a second example of a microaggression that Jane committed against me before she even became my manager, and not a subtle one either. I discussed this extensively with my food service manager, Anne, at the time; she knew something was wrong but had no explanations for it either. Critical race theory was such a new concept in 1995, but today these behaviors would be seen for what they were: very demeaning. As my manager, Jane ignored all of my achievements over the past eight years; she refused to accept that someone Black was intelligent and her equal.

For my first meeting with Jane as my new boss, I prepared a few examples of the dietitians' many achievements. I had concerns that she would know that I had applied for the job that she now held. She hadn't applied for the position; it turns out she had been put in the position by senior management. I am a dietitian and therefore was already familiar with the many food service programs and initiatives in which we were involved. I also had many relevant networking contacts. I was concerned that this might intimidate her. I thought I should reassure her that I didn't really want her job, and that I would be willing to help her with any projects for which she might need my expertise and assistance.

We were booked for an hour meeting. I laid out the binders of the projects the clinical dietitians had undertaken on the desk and went over them with her. Towards the end of the meeting, I broached the subject of my having applied for the job she now held and said that I hadn't really wanted it, and that I hoped she would let me help her and not be intimidated by my expertise.

The following week, my new manager, Jane, set up another meeting with me, this time in my office. When she entered the room, she did not sit down, and her first words to me were, "I shoot from the hip. Believe me, I will never be intimidated by you." Oh no, why had I used the word "intimidate?" She had obviously stopped listening to me after that; did she also hear what I had said about my willingness to help her? Critical race theory supports the reasons for her white anger: I had the audacity to suggest that a Black woman could intimidate her, a white woman. She put me in my place with as negative a response as she could.

She then began to tell me about the problems she had with me. "The only reason you were kept on was so that you could change a variety of things about your personality; the way you talk is in need of change. You use your hands a lot. Our meeting last week was a disaster." She said that she had heard from many other nurse managers in the hospital that I had problems that needed to be corrected. At our meeting the previous week I had said I would like, in my new role, to be able to sit on a few more hospital committees. About this, she said, "You will not be chosen to sit on more committees because you are ineffective." I want to point out that this meeting occurred the second week that she was my manager. Her behaviour to me was done in private, just between us. This is how she continued to belittle me. This was also the start of her making me invisible. There were many examples of microaggressions and microinvalidations at this meeting.

I was shocked and perplexed. Was this her agenda, or the agenda of upper management? What she said to me didn't make sense. My vice president had said nothing to me about my personality or the way I communicated, and even if he had said something about this to her, why wouldn't they have just fired me along with the other clinical managers who had lost their jobs that day? The way I talked? Was it my island accent? Was I too expressive? I realize now, as I explore critical race theory that I had many traits that were intimidating to a white woman. CRT says that white people are socialized to see Black women as the "nanny" and "Aunt Jemima," not strong and outspoken.

I thought back over the previous eight years. My job had not brought me into much contact with nurse managers; our paths just didn't cross. How could they have an opinion about problems

I might have? What problems? If I am ineffective on committees, then on which committees, and who had said this anyway? I realize in retrospect that over the past eight years my manager had presented her stereotypes of me to the nurse managers - who were her colleagues, after all. There had been eight years of racialization of who they perceived I was; many of the nursing managers had never even met me. I spent a sleepless night. My fears about my new manager kept returning. It had only been a week. I did not have any optimism about being able to win her over.

The next day I set up a meeting with the head of human resources to get some feedback about my interview for the manager's position. I wanted to determine if there were specific attributes that had been noted in the interview that resulted in me not getting the position. I needed to know this so I could prepare myself for management positions that may come up in the future. I also couldn't get past the fact of how inappropriate and unconstructive my new manager's comments had been.

I began the meeting by asking the manager of human resources what I could do to improve my chances of being hired for a management position in the future. He suggested I could sit on more committees. He also mentioned my lack of experience in working with unionized staff and how I might overcome this. We also discussed the general direction the hospital was taking with this restructuring and downsizing. Then I asked him directly if there were specific things that had been noted that I should work on improving. He said that upper management was generally impressed with my portfolio and that I had prepared well for the management position interview, but that most of my committee experience had been within my professional association and that I needed more in-house, hospital committee experience. On that note we ended the meeting.

I was encouraged by that meeting. I was relieved to hear that upper management still had a positive impression of my abilities. But the meeting hadn't told me anything about any of the concerns expressed by my new manager. I knew my future with her would be a challenge, but I told myself that if she can articulate specifically what it is she wants me to change I will try. I had spent 18 years building a successful reputation in my career, and I was confident that I could overcome this current adversity.

I must now relate the many initiatives that I undertook over the next several months to change who I was, how I was perceived, and to expand the value that I added to the hospital and its mission and vision. I actually thought that I could change my personality enough to meet my new manager's demands. Parallel to this was the business development side of my new job. I excelled in the many business initiatives that I had already successfully implemented. I consider myself an entrepreneur and was excited to be given this mandate. In spite of these successes, I was not judged on job performance by my new manager, but on who I was: a West Indian with an accent who was overly expressive, too friendly, and who couldn't change.

I really was on a path that led to my destruction. My new manager was the destroyer. I was not like her - I couldn't be - and she was going to use that to knock me down. Here she was, using her white privilege and unconscious/implicit bias, to defeat any efforts and changes that I put forward. Unconscious bias is often defined as prejudice or unsupported judgments in favor of or against one thing, person, or group as compared to another, in a way that is usually considered unfair. This fits what happened with my new manager exactly.

Unconscious biases are based on social stereotypes about certain groups of people that individuals form outside their own conscious awareness. Everyone holds unconscious beliefs about various social groups, and these biases stem from one's tendency to organize social worlds and people by categorizing them according to stereotypes. Unconscious bias can be dealt with or minimized if acknowledged, but Jane did not acknowledge that her behaviour was due to biases she held. Her assessments were accurate, she believed, and that was all there was to it.

So what did I do? I set up a meeting with educational services, my only resource at the hospital that could potentially help me develop strategies that I could use. At that first meeting, I shared with Peter, the educational services consultant, what my new manager had said I needed to change, along with my questions and responses to her criticisms:

- My manager, Jane, said that I referred to the dietitians as "my" dietitians and "my peers" and that I was too friendly with them. This had resulted in my not being objective. I suggested to her that what she observed as familiarity was cultural, very West Indian, and I thought it enriched my management style rather than hindered it. She didn't agree. Then she asked what personal things I discussed with my staff. I said there was one dietitian, Claire, who had kids my age, and that I liked her perspective on child rearing but I didn't see the purpose of the question so I didn't elaborate.

- My manager, Jane, said that I was "exclusionary" because I hadn't invited the food service supervisors to the Christmas party that I held annually for all of my staff. I corrected my manager on this and told her that I had invited them all, and only one had declined. I couldn't see how else I could deal with this negative misinformation.

I shared with the educational services consultant, Peter, that the main area that I was really concerned about and needed guidance on was the new surveillance my manager had set up to observe my behaviour and measure my attitude. At our weekly meetings my manager had a food service supervisor present who would monitor every response I made and rate my responses on a scale of 1-5. At the end of each meeting my ratings would be reported. My manager would also do her own assessment of everything I had said and would add any negative feedback that the food service supervisor might have missed.

I sat on one hospital committee and my manager had appointed a nurse on that committee to report back to her all my responses at meetings and to do a similar rating on the usefulness of my contributions. The same thing happened at my dietitians' meetings. My manager appointed a dietitian to note everything I said, to assess it, and to report back to her. I should say that one of the dietitians on my team had always been a bit insecure about her relationship with me and the team, and of course, this was the dietitian my manager chose to report to her. My manager had also cancelled my meetings on business development with my VP, Julian. My manager told the VP that she would report my progress to him.

The educational services consultant, Peter, stated the danger of my manager thinking that she could observe "attitude." We both knew, from the literature and from management experience that it is difficult to measure attitudes and feelings as well as determine if or when employee's feelings have changed without using clear and validated behavioural scales. Critical race theory supports that my manager's behavior and her descriptions of what she wanted changed were deep-rooted Black stereotypes of the aggressive, loud, rude and pushy Black woman. There would be nothing I could do for her to change her interpretation of my attitude.

Today, twenty-five years later, I would hope that an educational services consultant would be able to name all of these behaviours as microaggressions, but at this time neither of us understood or had knowledge or access to the research on microaggressions. Although the term was coined in 1970, it wasn't until the 21st century that the term has been applied. At the time, I was still thinking that if I changed specific aspects of my behaviour that

I could fall under my new manager's radar. I didn't realize that I was fighting a losing battle.

The educational services consultant expressed his concerns about the predicament I was in and thought the next step would be to see if we could get my manager to articulate specific behaviours instead of attitudes. He said he hoped he would be able to help me, but that if my manager continued to interpret attitudes that she perceived as wrong then I was heading for disaster. Of course, I was discouraged by this feedback. The consultant said he knew my manager would not be open to feedback about herself, so it was up to me to be alert at all times.

The consultant, Peter, offered to set up a meeting with my manager and me to discuss the feedback process. He also thought that another solution might be to set up team building exercises for the food service supervisors, the registered dietitian in charge of our computer systems, my manager and myself. I was encouraged by this suggestion.

Before these team building sessions began, however, I found out that my manager had informed the food service team that the reason for the team building exercise was to "get me to change." They were all OK with this; the exercise was to solve my attitude problems. She said to them that it was my "team mindedness" that had to "come around." I was in disbelief. She was so confident that she was right. I hope that in today's work environments there are support people who can intervene in this type of behaviour, but I am not sure.

The educational services consultant admitted that these sessions would be a challenge; he didn't understand what my manager meant by "team mindedness" and for a consultant whose main work was to teach team development to hospital work teams, this was saying something! I have always been a team player. The consultant, Peter, told me that he thought my leadership skills with the dietitians and with my staff were exceptional. I was open and sharing and receptive to each of the dietitian's needs. I created a balance between home and work life. The group was cohesive. He said that in terms of my communication patterns, I had been successful in leading my team for the past eight years and had been a contributing participant on other hospital teams. I am a warm person. I use stories to illustrate. He told me that he saw my communication style was based on my personality and that it was also a "cultural thing," not a detriment.

I was not sure if I could meet my manager's unclear standards on personality change, so I did what I thought would result in acceptance: I worked overtime on all my projects. I brainstormed on what I could do for my manager. I offered to complete two projects for her: an analysis of the cook-chill system and preparing questions for her food service supervisor interviews. She was pleased with these suggestions and I spent the weekend working on them. When I presented my work to her, she complemented me on work well done.

So far, I have highlighted my significant, mostly negative interactions with my manager and the food service staff. I should also note that my work performance in my regular duties continued at a high level of excellence. Each month, I established goals and at the end of that month I prepared a summary of what I had achieved for my manager, Jane. Here is an example of one month's report:

November:
Business Development:
- Negotiated, reviewed and signed a new vending contract
- Needs assessment survey for out-patient clinic completed and results analyzed
- Food and beverage out-patient interview survey designed
- Assessed Point of Sale terminal vs Access Cashless Point of Sale Terminal

Clinical
- Attended accreditation telemedicine with Clinical managers
- Established a new recording system on MIS for MOH
- Worked with Endo team to reorganize the area
- Attended five formal performance management meetings to monitor research and patient care goals.

Other
- Summarized and presented ADA conference to the leadership team
- Monitored the development of a training manual for diet clerks
- Established new clerical responsibilities for diet clerks
- Organized and participated in training on meeting skills for diet technicians and diet clerks with a trainer.

This is just a snapshot of one month's activity. Every month was similar. In spite of my manager's focus on improving my lack of "team mindedness," my work performance remained stellar.

To her credit, my manager did give me some positive feedback on occasion. I did receive some "thank you" emails from my manager for my work performance, for example "Just wanted to thank you for your hard work on the budget. I had a chance to review it thoroughly last night and was very impressed. It was well thought through and clearly presented." She also complimented me on my report on my dietitians' year-end accomplishments, self-directed work teams and on automation, and on the many other projects in which I was involved. She even said that the trainer commented positively on my communication skills.

One of my business development projects was introducing a "cashless card" in the cafeteria. Staff would be able to use this card to purchase food. The literature clearly supported an increase in point of sale purchases. This would be deducted from the staff's pay on a biweekly basis. By far, the biggest financial benefit I saw was negotiating with the university to designate our cafeteria as one of the choices for food that students could use. Why would food services at the university do this? The reason was that our food services had just finished a major project completing a nutrient analysis of many foods. The university wanted this. I knew the manager of food services at the university and because of a good professional relationship he was willing to make the trade.

As you will see, despite stellar performances on the many projects that I was challenged with, it would only take one perceived mishap for my hard work to be cancelled. I finished writing the final report on cashless cards a week before my manager fired me. She thought all she needed was my report in order to implement the cashless card. After being fired, I found out that she wasn't successful in implementing this new program; there were so many other steps in implementation beyond the report. One thing she didn't have yet was hospital staff buy-in, an essential component. I had planned to be at the entrance of the cafeteria for weeks where I would sell the card in person. I certainly had the outgoing personality and the right attitude to do this. My manager did not, nor did she see this as part of her role.

In May of 1995 my manager gathered the leadership team together to announce that our hospital and another local teaching hospital were looking into a merger. Their decision would be made in thirty days. They wanted the two food service departments at both hospitals to work together. Our food service team had a very negative reaction to this news. I tried to see things in a more positive light and said we had to try and work together with the team from the other hospital.

That night, a friend and colleague from the other hospital, Hanna, phoned me. We talked positively about the merger and gave it a positive spin. She said she thought our CEO would get the joint CEO position because their CEO was at retirement age.

I said to Hanna that I would understand if at some point in the future she didn't think it wise for us to talk to each other like this.

Our manager, Jane, announced another meeting the next day to discuss the merger. At this point the team was even more paranoid. They all shared concerns about losing their jobs. I was still positive. One of the supervisors asked me if I was not concerned about losing my job. I shared that I thought the clinical nutrition manager at the other hospital would likely get the position over me, because she had her master's degree, which I did not, and that was a requirement for running the dietetic internship program. I discussed the bigger picture. I said I thought the merger would use Ministry of Health dollars more efficiently.

The discussion turned to what we could do to position ourselves in a positive way. We decided that we needed information from other users on the cost of cook-chill (a method of food preparation process in which foods are chilled rapidly and reheated as required) and the costs of outsourcing. A number of people expressed the opinion that we should contact a variety of other cook-chill operations to ask about their costs. The hospital we were looking at merging with already had the cook-chill system in place, so I suggested that we just ask them what their costs were. This resulted in a very negative response. The team didn't think they would share this information with us. I said I had shared information with the other hospital before, as they had with me, and that I would be willing to ask. After all, administration said they expected us to work together. Unfortunately, I also shared that I had talked with my friend and colleague at the other hospital the night before about the merger. My boss exploded! She said that by my talking to Hanna I had chosen Hanna over her. I apologized profusely, wishing that I hadn't divulged any information. I said I hadn't made any choice of Hanna over my manager and that I wouldn't chat with Hanna again.

I didn't sleep that night, so I decided that the best thing to do was to meet with my manager again to reassure her. The meeting didn't go well. She finally had something she could use to fire me. All my hard work didn't really mean a thing when you analyzed it. After all, she did tell me, "I shoot from the hip." Despite the extensive research, analysis and planning I put into all my work.

My boss acted fast. Two days later I was summoned to our vice president's Julian's office. He looked at me apologetically. I was being given a settlement, "terminated without cause," as they used the term. The reason given was restructuring, and I was offered a good package. My services just weren't needed anymore. I was given a few days to go through my office and pack up. My VP's hands were tied; he didn't even know if his job would survive the merger. I have since referred to this as "being fired". Call it what it was.

My manager, Jane, said she didn't trust me anymore. The fact was she never did. I thought back to our second meeting and all the undermining she had done since she started. This was what she had planned to do from the beginning. I had finally given her a reason she could use with administration. She had presented the VP, Julian, with the file she had kept on my communication skills and on my lack of "team mindedness," and her perception of my cultural problems. She hadn't provided my monthly achievements, her positive feedback to me, or the fact that I had worked so hard to try and be what she wanted - without any support from her.

News travelled quickly. I had a few of my staff crying in my office. I decided to leave that day. I phoned my husband and he came to pick me up. I packed up all of what I wanted from my office and left.

I should end on a positive note. I cannot count the many supportive calls I received from all levels of management, my former vice presidents, doctors and other managers I had worked with. My staff had a huge farewell party for me. It was attended by the retired vice president of nursing, many managers, and senior staff, and every one of my clinical nutrition staff. This level of acknowledgement was very gratifying and reinforced the unfairness of what had happened to me. One of the benefits I was given was to have an outplacement counsellor from an impressive company, paid for by the hospital. This was apparently one of the perks of being let go "without cause." She played a significant role in my transition to university. She shared with me that I was the only person for whom she has ever been asked by the hospital to have a follow up session with their staff to help them adjust to their loss of their manager. Kathleen has since become a good friend and my mentor for the past twenty-five years.

One incident that reinforces the unfairness of my firing came in a phone call from one of the food service supervisors from my manager's team. Apparently, she had put my firing to a vote of her six supervisors, three voted for me to stay and three voted against me, and my manager broke the tie. Well this food service supervisor felt so guilty of voting for my dismissal that she went to counselling to come to terms with her unfair decision. One of the ways her therapist suggested she get closure was to call me and confess. I just listened.

I should add as well that my manager, Jane, was fired six months after I left. I received many calls from former colleagues wanting to share this information with me. Although I should have felt vindicated, it was interesting that I didn't really get any comfort from the news. I just didn't care. By this time I had completed the fall semester of my MBA program at the University of Guelph and was nicely settled in. I had moved on.

Chapter 11

Professional and Personal Development Employment, Equity, Diversity and Race

In my professional life I have spent a great deal of time on career development. In my two previous jobs I had continuously improved my clinical skills. I completed a university diploma in Business Administration. My job at Ultra Care, where I managed dozens of employees, made me concentrate on the best ways to hire people to create a high functioning team. I wanted to continue to improve my management skills. I was interested in many aspects of management but especially in hiring and interviewing. There was more being written about fairness in interviewing and behavioural interviewing techniques. I recognized that there were biases inherent in hiring employees who were "similar to me." I concentrated instead on hiring a more diverse staff, in terms of skills, gender and personality. In my studies and personal development, I learned the many benefits of a diverse team.

Myers Briggs became very popular in the 1980's, not only to understand your own personality but also to understand how you might adapt your personality to work with people who are different from you. I remember a workshop that included many managers from Ultra Care and the surrounding areas. We completed a

Myers Briggs assessment and were divided into groups of similar personality types. The exercise asked us as groups to say what we would do if we won a million dollars. The extroverts said that they would get together with their closest friends, fly to a tropical island and have a big party. The introverts were horrified at this. They wanted to go away by themselves or maybe with a couple of close friends to a quiet secluded place where they could read and relax.

What this exercise tried to show us was that within any team there are many different personality types that approach problems in different ways. It is not about right or wrong, but about how different personality types collaborate. At work I tried to put this information into practice when there was conflict between my staff. I would discuss issues and personalities with them, look at problem-solving techniques, and coach them to help them solve their specific problems themselves, using new skills. I was helped in this at Ultra Care by our excellent educational services department.

In my management role I was responsible for problem-solving and conflict resolution between my staff and other colleagues. I attended workshops where I explored my personality and how I affected others. I learned to interpret any negative encounters or conflicts I had with others as being related to how my personality interacted with theirs, i.e. the conflicts were due, I thought, to behavioural issues, not due to race. In a work setting I thought it was necessary to try to understand how I might best adjust my behaviour to be able to work better with the other person.

I know there is some disagreement with the validity of Myers Briggs. This negativity is mainly focused on the use of this tool as the final decision maker in the hiring process. I agree with this criticism up to a point, but I think Myers Briggs is a highly useful tool for helping individuals understand themselves and how we interact with others who have different personality orientations.

In Myers Briggs, I am an ENFP, Extroverted, Intuitive, Feeling, and Perceptive. ENFP's are referred to as "champion" personalities because of their enthusiasm for helping others. They are enthusiastic and independent. ENFP's are a bit less common; apparently only 8% of the total US population is ENFP. They are attracted to a challenge, both imaginative and original. They are future-focused, people-centered, love new ideas, are warm, passionate people, and are typically expressive communicators, using wit, humor, and language to create engaging stories. They have a strong artistic side. They engage anyone in a conversation at the drop of a hat, whether casually or collaborating in the workplace. ENFP's have tendencies to leadership and to assume positions of leadership readily and instinctively.

Weaknesses of ENFP's include hypersensitivity, which may result in perceiving bad intentions that do not really exist; they are endlessly creative and capable of filling a thousand days with a thousand ideas but they need to engage others for following through; their bubbly energetic style doesn't mesh well with introverts; and they pay too much attention to the opinions of others.

The opposite of an ENFP is an ISTJ: Introvert, Sensing, Thinking, Judgmental. Working with an ISTJ personality would be the most difficult personality for me to work with so I studied them the most. ISTJ's tend to be practical, logical, and have an unwavering commitment to duty. They take pride in their work and have a serious, no-nonsense air about them. They are calm, stable, cautious, and methodical. If they say they are going to do something, they mean it. As an introvert, they prefer to work alone and prefer to get things done rather than chatting with others. They are definitely not touchy-feely. They give practical advice over sympathy. They are direct and blunt, self-sufficient, and can come across as insensitive and have a stubborn streak. Unexpected changes bother them. Rules matter.

Communicating is a challenge between ENFPs and ISTJs. The ISTJ communicates in a straightforward, concrete way, focused on facts and real experiences, while ENFP's communicate in an abstract, theoretical way because they focus on making connections and interpreting what they see. Sometimes it seems that ENFP's and ISTJ's are speaking different languages.

I thought my manager at Ultra Care was probably an ISTJ personality, so I tried very hard to adjust some of my personality to her. She made it clear, however, that she thought my personality was the problem, and that she saw my differences from her as the problem, and that I was the one in the wrong. She repeatedly emphasized that I had to be more succinct in all my communication. This was the opposite to how I brainstormed to achieve more creative solutions, so she would spend time criticizing everything I said! At Ultra Care, to achieve this mindset, I would spend at least a half hour in the hospital chapel visualizing our meeting and verbally practicing how I would answer her questions succinctly.

When I reflect now on the problem between my manager and myself at Ultra Care, I see that although Myers Briggs was helpful in understanding how different she and I were, I now think using personality differences to analyze her antagonism to me was too simplistic. That is why my behaviour changes didn't work. My current understanding of her antagonistic behaviour towards me is more informed by the concepts of microinvalidation and microaggression. I will define microaggressions next, it is a difficult concept to recognize and understand initially, but I will give examples of this behaviour to illustrate its meaning.

Microaggressions are everyday verbal, nonverbal, and environmental slights, snubs, or insults, whether intentional or unintentional, which communicate hostile, derogatory, or negative messages to target persons based solely upon their marginalized group membership. In my case, the marginalized character was race. The significance of these microaggressions is how covert they were. "I shoot from the hip." These were words I can never forget, mainly because of how helpless they made me feel. These words were delivered to me in private, behind a closed door. It was very intentionally delivered and meant to demean me. The fact that I could not tell anyone is what made me feel helpless. Their significance is in their cumulative effect, which was huge.

There are sub-definitions of microaggression and the one I think closest to what I experienced at Ultra Care, and in my next workplace at Cornerstone Hospital in Springfield, was microinvalidation. Microinvalidations are communications that exclude, negate, or nullify the thoughts, feelings, perceptions or experiential reality of a person of color. The behaviour of my manager at Ultra Care fits this definition in many ways. She tried to make me invisible by controlling the committees I sat on and the one major committee that I sat on she had everything I said monitored and assessed by a nurse who was on the same committee. Even at our small department meetings she had one of the team members evaluate every word I said and rate my responses from one to five. She even controlled my dietitians' meetings by eliminating me as the chair and then having a stooge report back to her. My meetings with my vice president, Julian, were cancelled and she reported to him for me. In every way she could, she tried to silence my voice.

Later, you will see again that my experiences at a later job in Cornerstone hospital were a series of well-planned microinvalidations. Keep this in mind when you read them. Critical race theory provides another interpretation: cultural narratives are used by whites to frame racialized groups.

When I was fired from Ultra Care, I went to see a lawyer who thought I had an excellent case based on discrimination. I chose, however, not to take Ultra Care to court and pursue a case based on racial discrimination. My consultation with this lawyer did give me the satisfaction of knowing that I had a case that a prestigious lawyer was convinced was winnable. I know I could have won the battle; but I think I would have lost the war. In the bigger picture, if I wanted to continue in my chosen but conservative profession, then I could not take my employer to court. I would be burning too many bridges. I should also share that I wasn't the first person that my manager unfairly fired from a racialized group. I received more than one call encouraging me to take my case to court from other colleagues. I didn't feel, however, that I wanted to try to right past wrongs; it was too late.

In the mid-1990's, diversity was an important topic in human resources. Many organizations in Canada were discussing the implications of creating diversity in the workplaces and how this would affect their hiring policies. I think back to how much I had grown and evolved in my assessment of racism in Canada and how it has affected me as a Black West Indian Canadian.

In 1969, as a teenager, when I immigrated to Canada, my analyses and knowledge were limited to the feelings that various events had produced in me. My reading between 1969 and into the 1970's was from novels by similar West Indian immigrants; people who felt like me and gave my feelings some validity. At University, I took third world politics and black history courses to increase my knowledge. In the 1980's I developed strategies to handle uncomfortable situations and inappropriate insults that were directed to me in jest. In my private life I avoided putting myself in uncomfortable situations as much as possible. I had a wide variety of white Canadian friends with whom I interacted on an equal basis. But was I equal? Race was not part of our discussions. Should it have been? Many of these friends said when I confided my experiences to them that, "When I look at you, I don't see your color."

Although this would affirm an acceptance of me as their friend, they did not understand that this was actually denying my ethnicity and the experiences that I had encountered because of my race. This discounting of my feelings in difficult situations usually led my white friends to find a variety of reasons why the encounter took place that had nothing to do with race. "They are just jealous of you," my friends might say. I have since come to see this reaction as "white fragility," the tendency among members of the dominant white cultural group to have a defensive, wounded, angry, or dismissive response to evidence of racism.

For the most part, white people, especially Canadians, see themselves as "raceless" because they see racism as something harsh and overt. Because many see themselves as liberal thinkers, it is easy for them to deny my feelings and this blocks the exploration of whether the negative behaviour that I have received could be racist. This "color blindness" is unhelpful as it prevents further analysis of situations where covert racism is present and occurring and therefore eliminates addressing possible solutions. Critical race theory offers some knowledge and understanding because it analyses racism historically, going back to slavery and the labels and stereotypes of Black people then. These labels and stereotypes still exist today.

It was in my work life that it became harder to discount race as a non-issue. Race became an issue for discussion in Ontario in 1993, after the election of Bob Rae as Premier, and his New Democratic Party's (i.e. socially democratic) government's policies on affirmative action. I had known about affirmative action from the 1970's when my brother tried to encourage me to move to the U.S. for greater job opportunities. At that time I didn't want a job where I was hired because of my race. I wanted to be hired on my abilities and potential only. In retrospect, I see that this was naïve, but in order to understand it at that time I read everything I could find on affirmative action.

The U.S. had been involved with affirmative action since 1961, when President Kennedy signed an executive order that stated that "employees are to be treated during their employment without regard to race, creed, color, or national origin." Canada's history with affirmative action was much shorter. It was in 1984 that a royal commission on employment equity established preferential treatment for four groups: women, racial minorities, persons with disabilities and aboriginal people. Canada's first

Employment Equity Act in 1986 distinguished itself from the U.S. quota approach, and instead introduced goals and timetables.

The rise and fall of employment equity legislation in Ontario closely followed the rise and fall of the Ontario New Democratic Party (NDP) government in the 1990s, and the subsequent election of the Ontario Progressive Conservatives. The Ontario NDP historically held a strong commitment to the development and implementation of employment equity policy. During its one term in office as the majority government under the Premiership of Bob Rae, the NDP implemented the *Act to Provide for Employment Equity for Aboriginal People, People with Disabilities, Members of Racial Minorities and Women.* This legislation was short-lived; it lasted only a year. It was removed in an atmosphere of extreme backlash upon the subsequent election of Mike Harris and the Progressive Conservatives to government in Ontario in 1995. In fact, Mike Harris won the election on a platform of opposing the legislation and saying that he would "kill the act."

In my personal life I was of course also a full-time mother. I would be remiss to not talk about how my three sons, born to a mixed race Trinidadian mother and a white Canadian father, were coping. I can admit that I was not successful in instilling my awareness of race to them, nor to the fact that they could be treated differently because of their mixed race. As my children, they were first generation Canadians - through and through, not immigrants! Their father was a fifth generation Canadian who did not understand race. They also lived in Greenville Ontario, in a predominantly white community at that time. They had an affluent upbringing. They grew up with nannies, ski club memberships, and southern vacations every year.

I did not become as vigilant as I needed to be with my boys until after the first incident with the law. My middle son, at ten years old, was skateboarding at the local strip mall with his best friend, a curly red-headed boy with freckles. One of the storeowners told them that they should leave and that it was against the law to skateboard there. My son's friend used some foul language and they both headed back to their public school. A short time later, the storeowner went to the school and identified my son as the only one who had broken the law and who had sworn at her. There was no mention about his red-headed friend. The police were called and they charged a ten-year-old kid! No first warning and then demanding an apology, or writing a letter, or being given a chore. We had to hire a lawyer and go to court. I wanted our lawyer to use race in his argument against this charge, but he wouldn't. He said he didn't believe race played a part in my son's arrest. The only argument he used against the storeowner was, "You didn't like his hair, did you?" My son was sporting an afro at the time. Really?

I was also unlucky at the time to have had a neighbour who was a law enforcement authority. She told another neighbour - who related it to me - when my boys were only seven and nine, that she would be seeing them in court when they were older. I am sure she smugly thought that her predictions were correct, but what came first, her way of thinking about mixed race kids or what eventually happened to them? Critical race theory would explain her racialized thinking: our legal institutions are inherently racist, or at least incapable at this point of being applied equally to all. I can say that our ability to pay for lawyers was a help. Wayne and I always went to interviews and talked to probation officers. When they met Wayne and me, they quickly discontinued our visits: the boys were not serious offenders and as probation officers they had more serious cases to contend with. I did find some of their questions to be odd, however. For example, I was asked, "Is your son cruel to animals; had he killed any cats?" "No," I replied, "He sleeps with our pet cat at night." I guess this is one of the typical questions to assess aggression in young offenders.

Another seemingly small incident really bothered me. My concerned neighbour called one evening to say that the previous evening my three boys were going from house to house ringing doorbells and running away. I questioned my sons about it. It turns out that it was only my middle son, and two of his white friends whom he had hosted for a sleepover. My other sons were not involved. I told this to my neighbour, and she insisted she knew what she and the neighbours saw. My reason for my sharing this here is that I am sure that if this incident had been more serious, then all three of my sons would have been identified. Misidentification is a common problem for whites when identifying Blacks and people of color.

Another incident occurred when my youngest son was only six, his brothers were twelve and fourteen. One day after school my youngest son came home to find no one home. My husband was delayed because of a doctor's appointment with both of my older sons while I was rushing home to Greenville from the University of Guelph. My youngest sons' instructions were clear if this occurred. There were three places where he was instructed to go. To the home of two friends who lived nearby or to The Slopes the ski club where his dad worked. Instead he was delighted for the opportunity to go to the home of the law enforcement authority to play with her son who was his age. They immediately called the Children's Aid Society. Thank goodness that I arrived home minutes after their call to receive a call from Children's Aid who were double checking before they sent a car to pick him up at the neighbours.

All I could think of after this incident was my shy six-year-old being traumatized after being taken away by the authorities and the long-term effects this experience would have had on him. His two brothers were both of babysitting age and were always at home with him after school. In spite of this, Children's Aid continued to call every few days to check if my sons were there. When I questioned this, I was told that they continued to get complaints from my neighbour that no one was home with my son. My older sons walked home and entered my house through the back door which was not visible to my neighbour.

Another neighbour suggested that I should go and explain my circumstances to my neighbour. I was taken aback by this suggestion. We were both adults, she hadn't come to me with her concerns. I wasn't going to explain anything to her. I believe now that this aggressive move was also race-related. She saw me as a black parent, an unfit mother. My dear six year old son was so confused after this. He would ask "mom can I only play with Ethan in the street? Can I go to Ethan's house ever again? What about at soccer practice, can I play with him then?" I decided to take the high ground. I said to my son he could talk and play with Ethan whenever he wanted to and could even call him up if he wished. This was an adult issue not something to burden a six-year-old with.

I should also share that my husband could not see a problem with what his mixed race sons could be facing with the law. He didn't understand racism. I had been attracted to aspects of this characteristic in terms of my relationship with Wayne, but felt the opposite when it came to denying the prejudice his sons received. This situation got worse instead of better. To my alarm I came home one evening to see my husband talking to a policeman in our living room. He had called the police to give them a bag of marijuana that he had found in the house. He had confiscated it and was giving it to the police to teach our son a lesson. The policeman said he wouldn't charge my son as the marijuana could have belonged to anyone in the house.

I was furious with Wayne. This incident was the greatest test to the stability of our marriage. "The cops aren't on our side I shouted!! WE have to solve this. The cops will just put them in jail." As a minor, my son was charged with possession after all and put on probation.

Chapter 12

Guelph, Ontario, 1995 - 1998: MBA, Job Hunting, Teaching

After I left the Ultra Care hospital in 1995 my direction was clear. I would pursue my long-term dream of returning to university to complete a master's degree. Just like I did twenty years earlier, I wanted to spend this time in a degree program that was going to stimulate my intellect and allow me to grow. I wanted to explore the area of team building and restructuring that I had just experienced. Management practice at Ultra Care originally had the correct goals, but when these goals were also based on saving the bottom line, everything collapsed into a lack of trust and one of simple survival. I wanted to explore these ideas. I applied to the University of Guelph to complete a master's degree in business administration (MBA), specializing in organizational behaviour.

Within the organizational behaviour program, I was able to choose topics for independent study. These could include studying topics such as trust in organizations, diversity, teamwork, and even Myers Briggs. My interest in employment equity, however, led me to choose diversity training as one of my areas of independent study. At the hospital a friend had given me a copy of a Canadian Conference Board report on diversity training. This was a study that produced some clear data on the essential components of diversity programs. My thesis advisor agreed to supervise me in my pursuing this as my independent study topic. My main MBA thesis topic was: *An Analysis of One Hospital's Team Based Training Initiative for Self-Directed Work Teams.*

The initial investigations in the area of my independent study led me to a heritage insurance company in Ontario, and to the diversity trainer hired to conduct diversity training there. His view of diversity training was that it looks at how differences in gender, age, race, culture, physical and mental disability, sexual orientation, nationality, religion, language, class, education, style, personality and family status can and sometimes do affect productivity and effectiveness in the workplace. This definition was broad and important because it included white males, a group who were feeling most threatened by the suggestion of quota systems and sensational headlines like "white males need not apply."

This insurance company had anticipated the compulsory training requirements of the Bob Rae NDP government and they were ahead of the game before this legislation was introduced by implementing their own diversity training program. The main questions that I really wanted to answer as I looked at diversity training were: could diversity training change behaviours and could this training change attitudes.

Sadly, my research concluded that although diversity training could change organizational behaviour, and it could result in a change in how an individual might act in a given situation, attitude - how the person thought about another person, their attitudes of race and color - these are characteristics that do not change easily, and it would take many years of diversity training to achieve changes in attitudes.

I was left, therefore, with the realization that attitude change could not be the goal of diversity training programs. Diversity programs were sold to companies by promoting that there were economic benefits to companies that implemented them.

They addressed bottom line issues such as higher employment productivity through retention of the best employees, and the fact that greater productivity would lead to improved customer satisfaction and loyalty.

Diversity training programs can take up to three years to be carried out. The first phase is increasing the awareness of senior management to the issues of diversity. The second phase involves compulsory skills training of all employees. The third and last phase looks at career planning and recruitment. Unfortunately, this insurance company did not continue its diversity training program after the legislation requiring it was removed following the election of the new Conservative government.

Despite the failure of the NDP government and its employment equity programs, my research and exploration of diversity had led me to new literature and discussions on race. One of the areas I explored was unconscious bias (or implicit bias). This is often defined as prejudice or unsupported judgments in favor of or against one thing, person, or group as compared to another, in a way that is usually considered unfair. I also continued my work on my main MBA major paper topic: self-directed work teams.

I had the opportunity to apply some of the research I was doing in my MBA when I was encouraged to apply for a very challenging job of amalgamating (merging) the food services departments of two independent hospitals in Georgetown, Ontario. One of the directors of a large food company attended presentations of current thesis papers by students at the University of Guelph. He was very interested in my presentation about self-directed work teams. I was invited to compete for a position as manager, food services, to lead the amalgamation of these hospitals' food services departments. By this time, I had completed my course work at Guelph and had nearly completed my major paper research at two hospitals in Toronto where I observed their training of self-directed work teams. The project would enable me to put my research into practice. So I applied for the position - and I got it! I fully intended that if I got the job, I would have to return to complete my major paper at Guelph.

The amalgamation went well. We saved the two hospitals $800,000! Management at both hospitals were pleased with how smooth the process went. We literally walked staff from one hospital to the other, a few blocks away, to take on their new roles. Of course the food company that had originally invited me to apply terminated my position, after the amalgamation, but that was fine with me. By that time I wasn't really needed anymore, and it had been an excellent learning experience.

I received positive reviews from the CEO and the Assistant Executive Director of the two hospitals:

> "Cecily was a pleasure to work with... She was able to accomplish a reduction in the food services budget while maintaining excellent staff relations..... She has a great ability to work with people .... I would recommend her for any leadership position requiring professionalism, management and people skills."

> "I would like to recognize the significant contribution you made ..... It was certainly exciting for me to see the results of your many hours of planning, preparation and training come together..... Your knowledge and leadership were critical to this project."

The experience of leading this project reinforced my perception of myself; a leader who could be visionary and see the bigger picture; of putting my ideas about self-directed work teams into practice. After being fired by Ultra Care, this project did a lot for my self-esteem. I knew I could lead. Having to fire staff in the cutbacks that were necessitated by the amalgamation did affect my empathetic nature, however. I made the cuts, but they were emotionally difficult.

I graduated from the University of Guelph in 1998. I received high marks for my major paper and very positive evaluations from my committee, but most of all I had grown exponentially. As I have already shared, I found the academic environment highly stimulating. I spent much of my time reading, discussing and exploring many ideas that I wouldn't have had time for if it wasn't for academia. Although I believe my firing from Ultra Care was based on racism, it had forced me to re-evaluate what was important to me. I had realized very quickly after being fired that I wanted to return to university to complete my master's degree; this had been a long-term goal of mine. I thought that higher learning would protect me in some way from my experience at Ultra Care. As you will see, how wrong I was!

After graduation I began to look for work. My MBA major paper was on the establishment of self-directed work teams and the training of multi-skilled service staff in food services. You can imagine my pleasant surprise, therefore, when I was asked to an interview for a job that involved training staff at a hotel in the Caribbean. They were interested in me because of my thesis and because their company had tried one training program in Barbados that hadn't gone well. As I understood from what they told me, it had gone poorly because of the culture differences between the trainers and the staff and the Canadian trainers' inability to understand some of the value systems and culture of the Bajan service staff.

My interview for the position was to be with two of the company's trainers and they wanted me to demonstrate how I could conduct a training session. This posed a bit of a dilemma. Train-the-trainer workshops are quite different from training frontline staff. How would I do this training session for two experienced trainers? Then I had an idea: I would teach them how to do something that they had never done before. At the time, one of my creative craft projects was making grape vine wreaths. I decided I would teach the two trainers how to make grape vine wreaths.

I filled a basket with two undecorated wreaths, dried flowers, ribbons, glue guns, scissors and all the materials I would need. When I arrived for the interview, I told them I was going to teach them how to make wreaths. Without going into too much detail, I got them to choose where they would hang their wreath, provided verbal instruction and demonstrated how to use the glue gun, I gave them suggestions on how to decorate their wreaths, and I gave them positive feedback, praise, and guidance. The trainers were so impressed with my training skills that I was hired on the spot. Unfortunately, this was a perfect job that just wasn't meant to be; the company didn't get the contract they were hoping for. It was to have been at a hotel in St. Kitts. They wanted me to wait and be available for the next contract, but I had to return to reality: I had to find a job. Although I did apply to a number of hotels, I saw that the salary was only two/thirds of what a professional dietitian would make. I decided to return to health care.

I began by applying for jobs anywhere in southern Ontario, including Toronto. My boys were eight, fourteen and sixteen now. I was working hard to restore some order at home. I started by insisting that the family all eat dinner together; we would all be home for a family meal and could interact as a family around the table. I returned to doing good home cooking of their favourite foods and many of the Trinidad dishes that my kids loved. Eventually all my boys were home at dinner time again, usually with a bunch of friends. I would come home to boxes of hamburgers being cooked on the BBQ for everyone. I tried to say that hamburgers were a meal not a snack after school, why didn't they prepare hot dogs or peanut butter sandwiches for snacks? When this didn't work, I bought some thinner hamburgers, only to come home to see them making hamburgers with two patties instead of one. I really didn't mind; I preferred my sons at home in our basement with their friends. I am called mum by many of these boys, now adults.

I applied to one hospital job in Greenville - not the same hospital I had been fired from - and also to another smaller hospital in a nearby town. I was more than qualified for both jobs but didn't get an interview for either one. It became apparent to me that the manager of food services, Emma, for the newly amalgamated hospitals in Greenville controlled the hiring for both these jobs and that she was blocking my applications.

To avoid being blocked by this same food services manager again, I applied for a clinical dietitian position in Ashford, Ontario that she didn't control. I did get an interview. It turned out that the manager in this hospital, Elizabeth, was the same dietitian whose maternity leave position I had taken at the beginning of my career. We knew each other and she was familiar with my work. The interview went well and she offered me the position. I decided to take the job. I needed the work, and since it was initially only a part-time position, I would be able to do some consulting on my days off.

After starting my new job, I found out that my new manager at Cornerstone hospital had been contacted by the food services manager Emma, who had blocked my other applications. My new manager, Elizabeth, said that she had been told by Emma that she shouldn't have hired me because I was really only after her job. The enmity of some people seems to know no bounds! This dietitian would continue to impose microaggressions from afar. In more than one instance she would question my knowledge and abilities.

Shortly after I had started my new part-time position at Cornerstone hospital, one of my colleagues, who taught the management courses at a nearby University left her position. I applied and was hired as a sessional instructor to teach two management courses. It was a nice fit for all the right reasons. So

Immigration, Race and Survival

I began to settle in, working as a clinical dietitian at Cornerstone hospital, and teaching management at the university.

I should also share some parallel changes in thought and the evolution of my understanding of race and acceptance, at this time. As I have mentioned I was a sessional instructor at a local university. I was very pleased to be able to teach management studies to students in the master's degree program. I selected relevant topics to teach and, as you can imagine, diversity was one of the topics I choose. These students were the future. They were going to be professionals who would be managers and they would be part of allied health teams in a variety of settings. Others would be opening their own businesses as entrepreneurs.

I would often use a guest speaker, Anita, when we were studying diversity; she was a colleague at the university and the international student advisor. She conducted three exercises, the first of which was "unpacking the white knapsack," well-known now as the tool that illustrates white privilege. Students were asked to stand in a line and step forwards or backwards depending on their answer to specific questions:

1. If your ancestors were forced to come to this country or forced to relocate from where they were living, either temporarily or permanently, or were restricted from living in a certain area, take one step backward.
2. If you feel that your primary ethnic identity is "Canadian" take one step forward.
3. If you were ever called names or ridiculed because of your race, ethnicity or class background, take one step backward.
4. If you were ever embarrassed or ashamed of your clothes, your house or your family car when growing up, take one step backward.
5. If you have immediate family members who are doctors, lawyers, or other professionals, take one step forward.

6. If most of your teachers shared your cultural background, take two steps forward.
7. If you ever tried to change your physical appearance, mannerisms, language or behaviour to avoid being judged or ridiculed, take one step backward.
8. If you studied the history and culture of your ethnic ancestors in elementary school and secondary school, take two steps forward.
9. If you started school speaking a language other than English take two steps backward.
10. If your family had more than fifty books in the house when you were growing up, take one step forward.
11. If you were taken to art galleries, museums or plays by your parents, take one step forward.
12. If you ever attended a private school or summer camp, take one step forward.
13. If you received less encouragement in academics or sports from your family or from teachers because of your gender, take one step backward.
14. I can do well in a challenging situation without being called a credit to my race.
15. I can criticize our government and talk about how much I disagree with its policies without being told to go back where I came from if I don't like it here.
16. I can be pretty sure that if I ask to talk to "the person in charge" I will be facing a person of my own skin color.
17. If a traffic cop pulls me over, or if Revenue Canada audits my tax return, I can be sure I haven't been singled out because of my race.
18. I can worry about racism, and support programs that promote racial equality, without being seen as self-interested or self-seeking.

19. I can take a job with an equal opportunity employer without having my coworkers on the job suspect that I got it because of my race.
20. If my day, or week, or year is going badly, I need not wonder if each negative situation has racial overtones.
21. I have grown up with role models for achievement, in a wide range of fields, that are members of my race.
22. I can walk onto a train, plane, cafeteria, or school room and find it easy to sit next to someone of my race.
23. I can choose blemish cover or bandages in "flesh" color and have them more or less match my skin.

Needless to say, at the end of the exercise many white students stood well-ahead of the visible minority students who often had moved many steps backward. The exercise made its point. Many whites do not see the advantages they have experienced because of their white privilege. What this exercise also showed to the white students was the difference in privilege conferred by economic class and background. It was an excellent demonstration for showing students that privilege was not equal.

As an interesting side note, again to show that not all cultures of color share the same challenges, I did the test myself. It showed me that I scored positively in many categories. As a child I had new and fashionable clothes, I had professional family members, my teachers shared my cultural background, I spoke English, we had more than fifty books, I visited art galleries and museums as a youth, I went to private school, and I received encouragement in academics and sports. This showed me what I understood at another level: I had class and socioeconomic privilege. This privilege would not, I think, have been possible for me in a country with a predominantly white population like Canada, the United States and Britain, but it was possible in Trinidad and the Caribbean where the population was predominantly Black.

This helped me understand two things: one, this may be why I am accepted so easily among my white friends. In many ways I was just like them; and two, it may also have been why I wasn't accepted as easily among some white managers in job settings, especially those that I interacted with on an equal basis. They unconsciously expected me to be more subservient. They either interpreted my behaviour in stereotypical ways, or they diminished my accomplishments. The literature on black women in the workplace reinforces that black women consciously tone down their behaviour so as not to be assessed in stereotypical ways as aggressive, bossy and angry. I didn't change my behaviour, I didn't see the need; in my circumstances I didn't think it would have made a difference.

This exercise made me think of my life in Trinidad. I did have social or class privilege there still. For example, when I returned to Trinidad, I never went into Port of Spain to the passport office to renew my passport. I just gave it to my uncle, Hugh Harris, my Auntie Anne's brother-in-law, who would return a new passport to me a few days later. Uncle Hughie was the permanent secretary, Ministry of Education and Culture in Trinidad at that time.

My sons didn't have privilege in Canada, however. I remember giving my son money to go to the mall across from his high school to purchase some school supplies, and he told me he couldn't because he was banned from the mall the first week of school. When I questioned him I realized that high school kids went across the street to hang out at the mall over their lunch hour and that my son had been singled out by a guard at the mall and banned. I was furious. I immediately went to the mall with him and found the guard. Blatantly, my son had been banned because he was a Black kid with an afro. The guard said he could come to the mall if I accompanied him. I said, NO he will shop by himself and unless he was banning all white school kids also, I didn't plan to restrict my son. This was a small incident between me and a security guard. I knew, however, I would not likely be able to use this approach with other authority figures such as the police.

I didn't have privilege in Canada. I had privilege in Trinidad but I would return to Canada with no privilege at all. An example of this was when I was returning from New Orleans back to Canada from a nutrition conference with some colleagues who worked with me at Ultra Care. When I renewed my Trinidad passport, I would take it to the Canadian passport office to add their stamp and the date in 1969, the year I became a "landed immigrant." On my return trip to Toronto Person Airport a young female immigration officer detained me. She demanded to see more evidence than the stamp in my passport.

After interrogating me she locked me in a room for half an hour. I tried to tell her my husband was waiting for me with my two sons who were just three and five years old and that my husband could verify my status. While I waited I wondered where I would be sent. I couldn't be returned to New Orleans, our point of origin, because I had no status in the United States. Would they just send me back to Trinidad after nineteen years in Canada? I was frantically looking through my handbag and found the slip of folded paper that duplicated what was written in my passport. I showed it to the immigration officer when she returned and I was finally allowed to go. My colleagues were nowhere in sight, happily on their way back home.

Another exercise we did in my management courses at the university was on "dimensions of culture." The premise of this exercise was to consider core dimensions when comparing cultural similarities or differences. An awareness of dimensions of culture helped me understand my present situation at Cornerstone Hospital, and also the perceived concerns that the manager at the Ultra Care had had with me.

The dimensions were:

- Time and Consciousness. What value do you put on the use of time and punctuality?
- Sense of Self and Space. Is it appropriate to touch someone during a conversation? How close should you stand?
- Communication and Language. What are appropriate topics of discussion? How do you use body language and hand gestures?
- Dress and Appearance. What type of clothing is appropriate? How important is appearance?
- Food and Eating Habits. Are there rules and rituals around food and mealtimes?
- Relationships. How important is your nuclear or extended family? What value is placed on titles, age?
- Values and Norms. What is more important, conformity or individualism?
- Beliefs and Attitudes. What is the role of religion or spirituality? How are gender roles defined?
- Mental Processes and Learning. Is thinking logical and linear, or holistic and lateral? What role does fate play?
- Work Habits and Practices. What value is placed on work? How are rewards based?

As with the first exercise, there were usually significant differences in cultural dimensions between the white students and the students of color, brown and Black and their ethnic backgrounds. This exercise identified very different values of how I thought compared to some of my white counterparts.

A third exercise was "understanding my culture," where you filled out a chart with examples of: family structure, ethnic background, religious background, class, gender group influences, geographic location, mother tongue, ability, and other influences. We would also examine the "seven assumptions of intercultural communication." As an example, assumption number 7: "every communication has both a content and a relationship dimension."

The discussion of this assumption always highlighted the fact that communication can be interpreted at two levels: what is said (content) and how it is said (relationship), and that different cultures vary with respect to the amount of emphasis they place on these two levels. When I did this exercise, I related it to the differences between my manager and myself at Ultra Care. It was very revealing. She had made no attempt to understand my culture. It wasn't hers, and she assessed that, therefore, I had to change. As I have said before, for me being Canadian doesn't mean giving up your identity and culture; immigrants enrich the Canadian mosaic with their culture while adapting to the predominant culture and becoming a Canadian.

Chapter 13

Ashford, Ontario, 1998 - 2011: Cornerstone Hospital

As it turned out, my job at Cornerstone hospital lasted for thirteen years. It was the last job before I took early retirement from hospitals in 2011. From my extensive research on supervision, I knew when I started that how well I related to my direct supervisor/manager would have a significant impact on my job satisfaction and retention. They had interviewed and hired me but it was important for me to assess if I was a good fit with my manager, Elizabeth. I had had a mixture of good and bad fits in my career so far. By this time I had worked in dietetics for over twenty years.

In my initial days at Cornerstone hospital I determined that my new manager, Elizabeth, would be a good fit. And it was a positive relationship for seven years, until my manager retired. Her replacement, unfortunately, was not a good fit, and the last five years of my position at Cornerstone hospital would be among the most challenging of my career.

In this relationship with my final manager, Lena, I will leave it up to the reader to assess whether or not the difficulty stemmed from covert racism on her part. I will share how I felt and how I interpret her behaviour.

At Cornerstone hospital, I was hired to work three days a week, running the outpatient clinic and the weight control program. This was a new challenge that I was very excited to explore. I also covered inpatients when the clinical inpatient dietitians were away. When I entered the inpatient environment, I could see right away how conservative this hospital was. There didn't appear to be anyone else of color or Black on staff. There were none among the allied health professionals, just a couple of the physicians. I began to develop concerns about the "false consensus bias" I might encounter. This is a bias where the staff that I would have to work with may think that their own opinions, attitudes, beliefs and judgements are right and any differences to their way of thinking are wrong. Directed at me, this would be a covert form of racism.

Little did I realize that my first incident would be overt. This occurred after a couple months on the job. I was quietly reading a chart in the nurse's station when a nurse approached me. She took the chart out of my hands and said in a stern voice, "You are not allowed to read charts." I introduced myself as one of the new dietitians on staff and one of the nurses whom I had already met and who had seen this interaction came to my defense. She asked the other nurse why she had grabbed the chart from me and that nurse replied, with no hint of an apology, "I thought she was from housekeeping." I have been told that I am a great dresser, and this day was no different. I was wearing a green suede pantsuit. I wasn't wearing a uniform or an outfit that could remotely resemble what the housekeeping staff wore. This nurse saw only my race, my color, and nothing else. I realized then that I would have some challenges here. Again, my race made me an outsider, so I realized I would have to be careful about how I carried myself.

My first few years went well. There were a few human resources issues where I didn't think I was treated fairly. For example, I was in a scheduled three days a week position, but I wasn't classified as permanent part time; I was classified as a casual worker. By common labour standards, a casual worker did not have any scheduled hours but could be called in for relief of full time staff. Casual staff also had the right to refuse an offered shift. Because I had outpatients scheduled daily, however, I did not have the right to refuse to come in. This wasn't a concern until I wanted to join the pension plan.

According to the human resources policies of the hospital, casual workers could not join the pension plan. I had no idea that human resources would not grant me this benefit; the only advantage to them was the fact that as a casual worker they could terminate my employment at any time. My position changed from three days a week to four a few months after I started. My extra day would be for diabetes education which was granted another day a week. After this change, I approached human resources about my classification misrepresentation and my status was changed to part time so I was able to contribute to the pension plan.

I had already realized that the culture at Cornerstone hospital was conservative and white, and that I was considered an outsider. This had manifested itself in many ways. At Ultra Care, all dietitians sat together at lunch. Because we were such a large group we often took up one or two tables. We had a rule: no discussions of patient care or other work issues; it was to be all fun and casual. We shared stories about our vacations, parties we'd been to, films we'd seen, and TV shows we were watching. Lunch was a welcome break we all looked forward to. For instance, we had one dietitian, an East Indian, whose grandmother had completed her astrological charts as a prelude to the process of finding out who her future husband should be. Needless to say, this was a pretty unusual and exciting sharing and I can remember how we all rushed down to the lunchroom to hear the next episode of this drama.

At Cornerstone hospital, however, there were only 3 dietitians, so we usually sat with some food service staff and other allied health professionals. The first indication of microinvalidation was at these lunch times. For instance, sometimes I would bring pictures from my latest vacation to share with them, but no one would want to look at them and in some cases they would push them back in my direction without a word. Other people, however, would bring their own pictures to share and they would be looked at by the other staff.

It became worse when the allied health group of discharge planners would actually get up and leave when I sat down to join them. Even my own dietitian colleagues began to exclude me from their conversations. As part of my work, I occasionally had to take referrals to the dietitian in an outpatient clinic. She would often make me stand next to her with the referral for a few minutes while she finished discussing last night's TV show. Eventually the diabetes nurse and dietitian stopped coming to lunch altogether to avoid joining me. When I asked them about this, they said they preferred to eat outside or in their office.

Despite this treatment by my co-workers, I did enjoy my actual work. I loved the outpatient clinic where I had total autonomy. I was always pleased when I would have some success with my weight control clients. I was able to develop my own program and I experimented with different approaches. I had a student complete a research project where she developed and administered a questionnaire that gathered data about the success of my program. I attended a conference of the Caribbean Association of Dietitians and Nutritionists and presented the findings of this research. I attended the conference on the coat tails of a professor at the University where I worked who also was a presenter. She let me stay in her room at no extra costs and obtained conference support for my passage to the West Indies. I didn't receive any support to attend the conference from Cornerstone hospital in which the research had been done. I didn't let this bother me, however, because I was always in my element in the academic world.

The other area I was interested in and for which I developed nutrition programs was gastroenterology. The gut fascinated me, especially the area of constipation and general gut health. Because I had success in treating patients with gut problems, I began to receive referrals from some physicians in the area. I was encouraged by this recognition. I didn't have to think about how conservative Cornerstone was and how some of my colleagues treated me. I only went to the hospital to cover the inpatient dietitians on occasion. After some time I also stopped going to the inpatient cafeteria altogether and began to walk over my lunch hour. I explored all the areas around my office within a thirty minute walk. Here again I got peace in these nature walks. There was a lovely lake and a large creek nearby where I would head for peaceful walks to reflect on my day so far and prepare me for what lay ahead.

But all good things do come to an end and things began to change with restructuring at Cornerstone around 2005. By now I had been at the hospital for seven years. I had already been through two restructuring programs at two different hospitals and I could not believe I would have to face the process a third time. One significant change for me was that the outpatient building in which I worked, a self-contained, standalone building across the street from the actual hospital, was sold, and my office and the outpatient clinic were moved into the main hospital. I still did my outpatient work but began to be assigned more inpatient hours as well.

I saw that there were a number of projects in inpatients that could benefit from professional practice development, but they would need additional time to do. I approached my dietitian manager, Elizabeth, about getting some additional hours in which to do this work. This was not a radical idea by any means; many hospitals had designated hours for a professional practice leader (PPL). The manager liked my idea and created a PPL position, one day every other week. As per human resources protocols, she had to offer the position to the most senior dietitian first, which she did. When the senior dietitian Cara declined the position, I was granted the PPL hours. I used some of these hours to attend meetings in Toronto with other PPL's. I brought professional recognition to Cornerstone hospital by developing protocols for enteral feeding, workload measurements and new assessment techniques like nutrition diagnosis and behavioural interviewing.

In addition to this, I was allowed to accept dietetic interns for clinical placements. I was surprised that mentoring interns on a regular basis wasn't a priority for the inpatient dietitians until then. I was allowed to take interns on one condition: I had to do the paperwork and make the connections with dietetics programs. So I had three stimulating areas of professional involvement: my outpatient clinic role, my role as the PPL, as well as my work in the mentorship and preceptorship of interns. My circle of professional responsibilities was complete when I was granted a position on the board of the College of Dietitians.

When I look at my career, the one area of responsibility that gave me the greatest satisfaction was mentorship. The challenge of teaching a student to apply book knowledge in a practical sense was deeply rewarding to me. In addition to interns I would mentor one student all summer. The student would sit at my spare desk and on a daily basis I would ask them to solve a difficult case that I encountered at rounds on the floors. They would research the case and then come up with a variety of solutions. We would then have an intellectual discussion of their solutions. These exercises were a growth experience for me as well as the student. I am sharing this to illustrate that my days were filled with satisfaction that distracted me from the bigger picture, the social reality of my work context.

After three years at Cornerstone hospital, I volunteered to represent my region at the College of Dietitians of Ontario (CDO). In the first couple of years I was a non-council member and for the next seven years I sat on council, three of those years as President. My work with the CDO made use of my management skills and my organizational behaviour experiences. I would say that every month there was another challenge or another project to fill some of the social void I experienced at work. At Cornerstone hospital, no one seemed to appreciate the projects I did, but when I was at CDO all of my work was appreciated and my value reinforced.

Cornerstone hospital's first round of restructuring wasn't enough for the Ministry of Health so they sent in their own consultants to streamline the hospital even further. At this point, my dietitian manager, Elizabeth, the one with whom I had a good fit, decided she would retire. A director, a nurse, became our acting clinical manager until a new manager could be hired. The acting manager, Edith, immediately eliminated my PPL hours and responsibilities. A number of negative experiences occurred under the acting manager in a short space of time. For most of our time reporting to her, she was too busy to meet with us. I saw her interactions with me as demeaning and "putting me in my place" so I decided to bide my time until we got our new manager.

I had discussed the interactions I'd had with our acting manager, Edith, with others, a few friends and colleagues, and they said to me that it seemed to them like it was due to racial prejudice. I had not arrived at the point, however, where I could see it as such. I knew if I had even verbalized her behaviour towards me as racial prejudice that I would be the one who would be challenged. Learning the meaning of microaggression some years later and reading about critical race theory validated the feelings I had at the time. Although I couldn't do anything about the behaviour when it had occurred, it gave me some understanding later.

After a few trying months with the acting director, Edith, the hospital appointed a new manager, Lena. This was 2006. The three dietitians, myself included, were introduced to her the next day. My initial assessment of her was positive; she made good eye contact and seemed genuine. She said that she wanted to understand the role of the clinical dietitian and some of the challenges we were facing. She promised that she would set up regular meetings with all three of us in the near future.

When she became my manager I felt very positive about making a new start. Very soon, however, microinvalidation behaviour started. Lena met with both of the other two dietitians but would not invite me, or set up a separate meeting with me. The other dietitians would tell me things that Lena had asked them about me and what they had said to her. What is baffling to me is that they thought that this was okay. I knew they felt that it gave them some power over me.

The next five years under this new manager proved to be the most stressful period of my career. I waited and waited but Lena never set up an appointment to see me. Instead, I received an email from her saying that she had met with the previous acting manager, Edith, and wanted to inform me that:

1. The hours required to provide nutritional service to inpatients at Ashford Hospital as a clinical dietitian are 0800-1600h Monday to Friday, statutory holidays excluded.
2. Flexing my time would require authorization.
3. No time owing and/or overtime could be incurred without authorization.
4. No professional practice leader hours would be available.
5. I would need to make my own arrangements for professional meetings, teaching commitments, and medical appointments.

Lena continued to correspond with me by email-only for the next two months. The emails were most often highly directive. There seemed to be a systematic approach for her trying to demean me as much as she could, to invalidate what I stood for. But I couldn't understand why. I knew at some level that it had to do with who I was, but I didn't understand yet that her behaviour towards me was based on a long-ingrained attitude of superiority over me because of my color, my Black face and ethnic background.

After I received Lena's email about my hours I still had a number of questions and issues, so I wrote her back. Regarding my work with the College of Dietitians of Ontario, I tried to clarify that for my time on the council of the CDO, permission had been given by my old food service manager, Elizabeth, and that permission had continued under the acting manager, Edith, for me to attend CDO council meetings five times per year. I wasn't covered at the hospital on those days; I just worked longer hours the day before and the day after to cover my workload. I always gave the travel honorarium I received from CDO to attend these meetings back to Cornerstone hospital and paid for my own transportation. I asked what arrangements we could make for me to attend CDO council meetings in the future. Regarding my teaching at the university, I clarified that I had taught there since 2000 and that my class was on Mondays from 4:30 to 7:00 pm. I asked if I could continue to work from 7:30 am to 3:30 pm on Mondays, so I could continue to teach.

Lena's response was an email in which she repeated the points she had made in her previous email. She added that, "Overtime cannot be incurred unless the work required is of an urgent nature and patient care cannot be delayed. My expectation is that you will re-evaluate your workload and delegate work to the dietary technician who is scheduled until 1700h. If this is not an option my expectation is that you contact me or my delegate as soon as you have analyzed your workload and if overtime may be incurred." She then listed her pager and extension numbers so I could contact her or the manager on call to authorize my overtime.

My manager's response to incurring overtime demonstrated her lack of knowledge and understanding of clinical nutrition work. Overtime was typically needed when our hospital received a patient who had been transferred from another hospital and who would need a tube feed or a parenteral nutrition order. Most often these patient transfers would occur at 4:30 pm and would require the dietitian to work overtime. Tube feed or parenteral nutrition orders were not consults that could be delegated to a diet technician. It had nothing to do with my organizational skills and how I dealt with my workload. My manager's persistence in not meeting with me resulted in this problem never being resolved. Lena was long gone at 4:30 pm and the manager on call would question why I was paging her to ask her a question with an obvious answer; of course go and assess the patient! It was embarrassing for me and I would often have to wait before my call to the manager on call was returned. Most often, I just did the assessment on my own time and did not claim overtime.

I asked my manager, Lena, for clarification on some flexing of hours when I had a doctor's appointment. I lived in Greenville, which was half an hour's drive and, depending on the location of the doctor's office, it might take even longer. Her response was that I should get a doctor in Ashford. This was an unrealistic solution that I would not be able to comply with. The suggestion that I should change my family doctor and my other specialists - allergist, cardiologist, etc. - to doctors in the small city was not only unrealistic but impossible.

Another point on this issue was that there were many staff at Cornerstone who lived out of town and commuted to work and who had their doctors there. My union rep told me that his manager let him flex his time when he had a doctor's appointment. It was apparent that there was a double standard, one for me, the only Black person at the hospital, and one for everyone else.

My role at the hospital changed further when, as part of the restructuring, I was told that the outpatient clinics would be closing. I sent an email to both my manager, Lena, and her director, Edith, asking for a meeting to discuss this transition. This seemed reasonable because there would be a number of issues to resolve. One issue that I was concerned about was that local doctors would need to be notified because they relied on the outpatient service. My manager, Lena, replied by email saying, "I have received your request to meet with us to discuss your new role. I would refer you to the two emails I sent about your work hours."

I had a hard time believing that my manager and her director thought that running and being in charge of a clinical specialty is only about scheduling. They were so focused on "putting me in my place" and invalidating who I was; I felt that they were willing to sacrifice patient care instead of contacting local doctors to inform them of the change.

In December of 2006, the hospital subscription to the online *Manual of Clinical Dietetics* came up for renewal. I sent the request for renewal to my manager letting her know that this manual provided the dietitians with evidence-based practice guidelines, best professional practices, and practitioner and consumer tools on a wide range of food and nutrition topics. Lena didn't reply and I got a second renewal notice. I was not sure if my manager's non-response was intentional or not, so I wrote another email asking her to renew the subscription. I should interject here that in normal circumstances a simple phone call should have sufficed for such a routine concern, but Lena had begun to not take my phone calls. She just never picked up her phone when I called. I had also been told by Lena in a subsequent email not to call her.

Regarding the renewal; I received a curt reply from my manager saying, "We have until late January 2007 to renew this subscription. I will review the information you have sent me." To this, I replied, "Thank you for your response. Some additional information: we do not have any current reference textbooks on nutrition in the hospital either. The two nutrition textbooks, one in outpatients and one in inpatients, are both out of date. It would be useful to purchase newer nutrition textbooks."

This was perhaps the only time I received a prompt response from her. Lena responded immediately, "Your tone in the email communications I have been receiving from you concern me. I feel it would be helpful to remind you of our hospital policy number 12.23 regarding respect and behaviour in the workplace.

I would like you to review this policy. When communicating by email it is expected that you act in a courteous and responsible manner. I refer to the two most recent email communications in which I am sensing hostility and a confrontational tone directed at me. This organization has performance criteria that emphasize teamwork, avoiding disruptive behaviours, and respect whenever and however you communicate. You are required to meet these expectations when communicating with me or any individual in the organization."

"Sensing hostility and a confrontational tone?" This was a *déjà vu*. Here is another nurse manager who thinks she can assess my attitude from email responses to her emails. I have discussed earlier how attitude cannot be adequately measured, nor can a manager determine if or when attitudes have changed. This interpretation of my manager to my passive emails, and her not allowing one-to-one communication was very troubling; this is an important construct of critical race theory: the angry Black woman narrative where if a Black woman complains, she is depicted as aggressive, loud, rude and pushy. This was a construct even the educated, articulate Michelle Obama faced from the media in the United States as the First Lady.

This narrative of the angry black woman would be repeated with Meghan Markle, the wife of Prince Harry, Duke of Sussex. Markle, a mixed race woman, was vilified by the tabloid media as a "bully" and depicted as aggressive. This narrative has been played out again and again against Black women.

I read Lena's emails over again. I found it hard to see where my two most recent emails showed that my behaviour was inappropriate; that my tone was not courteous and showed a lack of responsibility; that they showed hostility; that I was confrontational; that they demonstrated that I was not a team player and that I was disruptive and not respectful. In fact, if I looked closely at her email, it would be easier to think she had been talking about herself!

Of course, I went back and reread all of my emails to her. I failed to find any instances where I was guilty of what she had accused me of. I thought to myself, 'Maybe she thinks a manager can talk down to an employee; maybe, for her, respect is a one-way street?' I know that without face-to-face communication, the recipient of an email can read tone of voice and negative body language into what is written. Because Lena had already decided that I was a problem employee, was she reading rudeness and aggression into my words? Maybe she wanted me to put on my "Aunt Jemima hat" and say, "Yes ma'am, no ma'am, more please, and thank you very much?"

The point is, I know that I was being polite and respectful. I also knew that I needed to meet with Lena. I became physically sick, I lost sleep, and I had a fender bender accident that was probably related to how tired I was. I did not know how to solve the problem of my manager refusing to meet with me. What I realize now is that meeting with her would not have changed her mind-set to me as a Black person.

I set up an appointment with a human resources representative to ask for guidance. When we met, I explained the situation and provided her with all of my manager's emails. She did not see a problem. The inability of white human resource employees to see race as a reason for how my manager Lena was treating me was also because she had no social construct in which to understand and view my situation. Her advice was for me to set up a meeting with my manager through her administrative assistant. Following her advice, I set up a meeting for the next day. When I arrived, my manager Lena was at her desk. She didn't ask me to sit down and instead, informed me that she hadn't accepted my appointment. I left broken.

I went back to human resources and explained what had happened. The HR rep said that she would talk to my manager. She set up an appointment for me. At this point it was later in December and the meeting had been set up for just before my

Christmas vacation. One afternoon, I passed the hospital gift shop and saw two, beautiful silver doves for sale. I went in and bought them. At the meeting with my manager I presented her with one of the doves saying that I hoped she would accept the gesture and that I came in peace. This illustrates my naiveté at this time in not seeing my manager's behaviour as related to race.

The meeting with my manager wasn't a great success. She stuck to her points on time and scheduling in the first email she had sent me when she started. I did, however, feel more peaceful after we met. I didn't know what I was experiencing at the time but when I look at her behaviour to me today, it fits the description of microinvalidation. Unfortunately, this would continue unabated for the five more years that she would be my manager.

As might have been expected, things didn't change much in the New Year, but at least I knew where I stood. I did begin to enjoy inpatient dietetics again, however. Outpatient clinics closed on December 31st. Inpatient medicine, surgery and ICU were my favorite floors. I dove into nutritional support in ICU. MD's for the most part trusted me, especially the surgeon who was the physician representative on my enteral nutrition protocol. He gave me permission to write orders for his patients. I was stimulated by the challenge and autonomy. As I have mentioned before, a dietitian's day is often very autonomous, and she is free to set her daily agenda. My contact with my manager was only for days off and scheduling so I really had no contact with her other than when I wanted to rearrange something in my schedule.

Although there was an almost entirely negative relationship with my manager, Cornerstone hospital had an amazing CEO. He devoted resources to teamwork and staff development throughout the restructuring process. He had even hired an outside company to do team training in every department from upper management to the service staff. Unfortunately, diversity was not their focus. I was so impressed with my CEO that I used him as a guest speaker for my management studies course at the university. No doubt some of my students would be working in hospitals that would be going through restructuring and his lecture opened a window into positive management skills.

In spite of the lack of recognition and support from my manager, I was always confident in my clinical skills. I was active in the College of Dietitians and reviewed the clinical nutrition literature regularly to identify best practices. I developed teaching tools to try and achieve behavioural change in patients – always a challenge. I mentored interns at the hospital and taught students at the university.

Unlike Ultra Care, where I worked before obtaining my master's degree, this job at Cornerstone hospital was different. Even if my manager, Lena, wanted to try to make a case about my clinical skills, a nurse could not assess a dietitian's competency. She would have to make a complaint to the College of Dietitians of Ontario, with evidence. The CDO would then have to appoint an assessor to come to the hospital to assess my competency. This would be a highly unlikely occurrence. I felt secure in my clinical skills and I had the confidence of many of the doctors in my abilities. I felt secure that they would support me if any complaint was made.

My CEO's focus was on "change" and he hired a company whose program was called *Awakening Intuition*. I was absolutely fascinated by this concept and wanted to be involved with what this program had to offer. The program was based on the premise:

"Leaders must be the change they want to see in the world". This is a quote from Ghandi and the program leader developed his whole program around this quote. He stated that his program's sessions were based on a number of "great truths," including:

- Culture is the "programming" of the organization (values, beliefs and behaviours), which distinguishes it from other organizations.

- Leaders drive culture. Culture plays "follow the leader."
- Transformation requires leaders to source courage, tenacity, compassion and a willingness to see with new eyes, moving leadership from good to great, to inspiring.

The consulting company announced that they would include four staff at Cornerstone to assist with the workshops. To be accepted you had to complete a questionnaire. I volunteered. My results showed very high intuition and I was chosen to be one of the four staff assisting their team. I should add that my manager could not object to my role as these consultants were approved by our CEO, but my manager mandated that I had to make up the time I spent working on this project. I did this gladly.

For the most part, I assisted by acting as an objective scribe, silently taking notes and then interpreting my observations at the end of each session with the consultant. One of the clear outcomes of this work was that there was a lack of trust felt by staff of management, especially nursing management. Some staff would ask, "Have management been to these workshops?" For many, there seemed to be a disconnect between what staff were experiencing in these sessions and the reality of daily work life. I felt similarly and couldn't understand how what I was experiencing in my team could exist in the same environment when we were trying to "awaken intuition."

Unfortunately, this program only completed the first part of its mandate, the "what needed changing" part. The "how to change" part never materialized. The project was abandoned when we received the Ministry of Health report on further restructuring. One of the results of this further restructuring was that they cut inpatient dietitians from two dietitians to one. It would have made more sense to only cut dietitian's hours down to one and a half dietitians, but this would have meant that they would have had to keep me on part-time, and they didn't want to do this, so they cut us down to one. Because the other dietitian was more senior than me, my position was eliminated. I was certainly familiar with this process! Other organizations cutting positions will do firings midweek and not on a Friday for consideration for the employee. There is also usually a counselor available either in-house or with an outside agency to give the employee some support. I was granted none of these courtesies. I met with the director, Edith, and my manager, Lena, and was told that my job was to be terminated in three weeks. I am sure this three week notice was given only because I was unionized and had to be given notice.

I knew the law from my MBA courses and my past management experience, so I asked them, didn't they need to offer the other dietitian, Cara, a package first since she was at retirement age? They said they would look into that. Also, I asked, if Cara didn't take the package, then didn't I, by union law, have to be contacted and be offered her job when she did eventually retire? They said they would look into that too. They asked if I was okay and I said I would be going to see my family doctor after I left them. I went down to my office. The other dietitian, Cara, and my diet technician, Cheryl, already knew what my meeting was about. Also, our tube feeding representative was waiting for me. I had forgotten that we had scheduled an appointment. He was a long-time colleague and said he could cancel but I said that since he was here already I would keep the meeting to get his update. I left at my usual time, 4:30pm.

You would not believe my shock when I returned to work on Monday. The director's administrative assistant told me that the director wanted to see me about having "padded" my time sheet. I was appalled. When I asked what it was about the director reminded me that on the day she fired me I had told her that I was leaving work and yet I had submitted a time sheet for a full day. I couldn't believe it! I explained to her about the meeting with the tube feeding representative, and I left her office in shock and dismay. It made me angry and hurt to think that even if I had worked an hour less after being told I was being terminated, that she thought it would be fitting to dock me an hours pay!

Because it was required by union contract, the senior dietitian, Cara, was offered a package. Over the next three weeks I would ask Cara if she had decided if she was accepting the package that was offered her for retirement. She kept me in the dark, saying she hadn't made up her mind as yet. I only found out days before I would have had to leave my position. She had made up her mind days earlier, but decided to keep me in the dark. She got a sweet package of over a year's full pay because she had worked in the same job for close to forty years. She would have been crazy not to take it. And I would be keeping my job! If my manager, Lena, and my director, Edith, had only cut the dietitian hours down to one and a half dietitians, and waited for the senior dietitian to retire, which I think she had planned to do, they would have saved the hospital thousands of dollars. But they were in such a rush to finally get rid of me, their plan backfired. Not only did they have to package the senior dietitian out, they had to keep me.

My manager, Lena, could not criticize my work in patient care until one day she received a complaint from the speech language pathologist (SLP). My pager went off; my manager was ordering me to come to her office immediately. I left the patient assessment I had been doing and as I made my way to my manager's office I was wondering, what now? She had apparently received a complaint that I had changed a swallowing patient's diet texture, an order that was strictly the role of the SLP. Although the patient did not have a negative reaction to the diet texture change, this was obviously a "turf issue," since diet texture changes were always the role of the SLP. Assessing whether a patient with a swallowing disorder would benefit from a diet texture change is certainly not outside the role of clinical dietitian, but the actual change order itself needs to be made by an SLP.

My manager was not on my side. She said she could present a complaint to the College of Dietitians that could result in my being disciplined. When I was a manager, and I got a complaint about one of my staff, I would do everything I could to support my staff until we got to the bottom of the complaint. I wasn't supported by my manager in this case. I couldn't remember the specific patient because the incident had happened about a month earlier. I asked my manager if I could investigate the complaint myself. She agreed, and I did. It turns out I hadn't made the change that the complaint was based on. The SLP who had made the complaint had been on vacation and had been covered that day by another SLP. It was the covering SLP who had made the change. The complaint was dropped, of course, but the lack of support I received from my manager still bothered me.

The following incident was another example of how my manager at Cornerstone hospital saw me as a dishonest person. This stereotyping of Blacks as dishonest is supported by my research and is a theme that has followed me throughout my working life. In this incident, my manager jumped to the conclusion that I had cheated on my time sheet. Dishonesty is one of the social constructs of critical race theory: Blacks are dishonest.

I had to go to the local courthouse to appeal a dangerous driving charge. On my way into work one morning, I had skidded lightly into the rear bumper of the car in front of me. Unfortunately, the car I had hit was the private car of a policeman. There was no damage to my car and very minor damage to the rear bumper of the policeman's car. The policeman felt compelled to charge me with dangerous driving, which includes a loss of three demerit points on your license. I decided I would fight the charge and went to court over my lunch hour to appeal. I was successful in my appeal – I didn't lose any demerit points – but the process took two hours instead of the one hour I got for lunch.

After returning to work, I therefore worked an extra hour at the end of the day to cover my time. I decided to email my manager to let her know about the adjustment of hours I had made. My manager responded by saying that because I had told her after the fact, I was being "dishonest." I pointed out to her that if my court appearance had only taken the hour I had expected, I wouldn't have had to tell her anything, and that I did not understand why dishonesty was the first thing that came to her mind. This dishonesty theme never went away and resurfaced on a number of occasions.

The CEO of Cornerstone hospital had mandated after restructuring that managers should meet regularly with their departmental teams. I was pleased to begin having regular team meetings with my manager. We began to meet over lunch on Wednesdays in the dietitians' office. The inpatient team consisted of my diet technician, my manager and me. My diet technician's main role was to counsel patients on simpler diets that I delegated to her, in addition to her main task of processing food services special diets on the computer.

In addition to assessment of clinical patients and teaching of special diets, I completed many special projects. One of the main projects I worked on was the development of the tube feeding and TPN protocol. This required establishing a multidisciplinary patient care team, extensive best practice literature reviews and consultation with the critical care dietitians at two teaching hospitals.

The Cornerstone hospital committee that oversaw my work on this project was very pleased with the final report and the proposed protocol. The last step was for my manager to take this protocol up the channels and have it approved. I would also be invited to do the final presentation to upper management. In what would prove to be the single greatest example of microinvalidation by my manager, she never followed through on this document's approval process in five years. To do this she would have to acknowledge my role. Not following through was an invalidation of who I was and the work I had done. The intensive care team and the teams on other medical floors continued to use my protocols as a "guideline" but because of my manager's microinvalidation, it was never adopted as a formal hospital protocol.

The final straw in this process of invalidation was when my manager announced that my projects took up too much time at meetings, and that I should give my diet technician Cheryl equal time. Diet technicians do not typically do any major projects and their work is often fairly routine and done at the delegation of the dietitian. So yes, it's true, most of the discussions at our team meetings were either me updating my manager, or the manager providing us with hospital updates. But if my manager wanted the diet tech to have equal time, I would satisfy her request.

I had run meetings my entire career. At that time I was President of the College of Dietitians, which followed *Roberts Rules of Order*, so I was well versed in preparing agendas. I therefore volunteered to complete a standardized agenda for our lunchtime meetings that delegated equal time to the three of us. I stopped explaining projects in detail to my manager. I still did the projects but would prepare a report document for her review. I was sure she didn't read any of these reports I gave her because she never asked me any questions about them. This would become obvious every so often.

I had decided to implement an advisory consulting program. This was an internship program that the College of Dietitians had recently developed. I wanted to train the first intern that I accepted myself at Cornerstone hospital, because I was confident in my personal training abilities. I should explain there is a difference between advising and training. I received no reimbursement for taking on this work. I shared the independent practicum guide, which stated what my role would be and that I would receive no reimbursement, with my manager at one of our weekly meetings. I gave her a copy of the guide to read. A few days after the intern started, one of the other dietitians - the formerly retired dietitian, Cara, now doing part-time coverage - told my manager that I was charging the intern a fee for his training at Cornerstone hospital.

Had my manager read the document I had shared with her or read the minutes from our team meeting where I had told her about this she would have understood my roles in the independent practicum process, and that I would not be receiving any reimbursement.

Instead, my manager sent the dietitian, Cara, who had misinformed her, to meet with me and to find out more. When we met, Cara proceeded to ask opaque questions. She first asked, "How much does an intern pay an advisor?" Not knowing where this was going I asked her if she was interested in becoming an advisor herself. The interrogation continued for about an hour. I finally asked her if my manager, Lena, had asked her to get these answers for her. She said yes. I then asked if she didn't feel uncomfortable being the stooge? She said our manager was her boss and she had to do what was asked of her. I thought at least that answer made it very clear where she stood. The next morning my manager called me. Just to be sure of my position, I sent her another copy of the minutes of our team meeting, the one at which I had given her the independent practicum guide. I also asked the registration manager of the College to confirm, in writing, what my roles were. I forwarded this email to my manager.

From past experience, I had known that Cara was antagonistic towards me. A year or so before her retirement she had come to my office and felt the need to tell me that we were very different people and that she didn't consider me a friend. At the time, I was hurt. I didn't understand why she had felt the need to tell me that. Even though she felt that way, she could have said nothing and wouldn't have created the antagonism that now existed. It was cruel and hurtful but she obviously could not display empathy to me, and my feelings were not considered. A year later, when Cara retired, I was put in charge of organizing some aspects of her retirement party. I asked other staff to donate pictures of Cara at work events and I made a collage of these pictures. Perhaps it was because I had made it, or because some of the pictures included ones of me and her, but she never took the collage home. Cara didn't even have the courtesy to take it with her and throw it out when she got home.

I see all this now as another case of continuing microaggression. Yes, I was different from her: she was white and I was Black. In her eyes and in my manager's this was reason enough for them to look for ways to devalue me, to feel superior to me, and to try and find fault with me. I somehow doubt either of them would think they treated me differently or were unkind. Critical race theory suggests that white people do not often feel empathy to Black people. I am sure that in her mind I was getting what I deserved.

My manager always wanted more respect. On one occasion, I had asked my manager via email, well in advance, for a vacation day off to attend a College of Dietitians meeting in Toronto. By four o'clock on the day before the meeting I still had not heard from my manager about my request. I had already emailed and left a couple of voice messages asking my manager if she had approved it. I certainly had no reason to think she wouldn't approve it. So I just assumed that she had forgotten or was too busy to respond to my earlier messages. I was pleased, therefore, when I left my office at four and saw my manager walking up the hallway ahead of me. I called out to her. She didn't turn around or answer. I continued to follow her and caught up with her at the door of the payroll office. She turned to me and demanded to know how I could be so disrespectful to call out her name in the hallway. She said that I had also been disrespectful in the past, and that she was heading to payroll to sign my request for the day off. "Do not let this ever happen again," she said.

So, again, she had "put me in my place." What could I say? Microaggressions have an economic, social and political advantage in the workplace. Blacks have historically been described as dishonest, lazy, untrustworthy, overbearing, loud, rude, pushy and aggressive. I had been characterized by many of these labels at Cornerstone. As I described earlier, even the intelligent, professional, outspoken Michelle Obama was often portrayed as an angry Black woman. I felt that I was being painted with the same brush.

Despite the frustrations I felt with my manager, I enjoyed my role as a dietitian. The majority of my daily responsibilities were performed autonomously and my contact with my manager was only when I had to get time off, approval of vacation time, or to deal with any human resources issues.

I would like to explore some of the other microaggressions I experienced at Cornerstone hospital. I know that the word microaggression can be difficult for many people to understand. Let me give you some examples. One clear microaggression is exclusion, and I experienced this in many instances. I was clearly a member of the "out group." The "in group" did everything to prevent me from being understood and accepted. They refused to socialize with me. They got up and left when I sat with them at lunch. When I tried to share my vacation pictures, they pushed them away. My manager would not meet with me.

Other microaggressions included: she repeatedly accused me of not respecting her; she accused me on more than one occasion of being dishonest; she would ask the other dietitians about me but would not meet with me directly; she discounted any of my expertise and refused to accept my accomplishments, for example, the presidency of the CDO. For a hospital as small as Cornerstone to have one of their staff become president of their college should have been prestigious but my manager was not prepared to acknowledge my position because it would place the spotlight on me. She also refused to follow through on the acceptance of the tube feeding and TPN guidelines as a protocol which I was instrumental in developing.

This is just a snapshot. You have read my experiences in their entirety. How did I continue to perform my job under these circumstances? It is well-documented that many workers have mental health issues and decreased job performance when they experience microaggressions. I think that I am very resilient. I am described by many as having a strong personality. I am confident and optimistic. I do not think I could have survived otherwise. I have discussed that I really loved my job. I think that I chose the ideal profession, a caring, helping profession where I received satisfaction from the nurturing of others.

One of the qualities of those in the helping professions is emotional resilience. I would go home after work and feel positive when I reflected on the one or two patients that I helped that day. Don't get me wrong, my manager's behaviour and that of some of my colleagues did affect my sleep. I used to believe that I was a poor sleeper, but I really am not – as I have discovered since I retired. My manager's behaviour towards me, however, did affect my sleep, but not yet to the extent that it was critical. It helped that I had a lot of joy from a very active life away from the hospital with my family and friends and my loving husband. As I said, I was resilient and have a firm belief that I should not spend a lot of time worrying about things I could not change. I had accepted after many years that my manager was not going to change, so I learned to live with her unacceptable behaviour towards me and I got my satisfaction in other ways.

We should never underestimate the importance of connection and love from family and friends. My strength came from my strong support system. I interacted with two sets of friends and their children as family. We did everything together and especially celebrated special occasions like Christmas, Easter and Thanksgiving. I had a group of five girlfriends in the city where I lived with whom I would get together for monthly dinners and birthday celebrations. I interacted with my family frequently, especially my brother and his children in the United States. These many outlets gave me strength to return to work weekly. I knew there was good in the world.

I didn't make a lot of close friends at Cornerstone hospital, just three that I have kept in touch with. By contrast, I had expanded my circle of close friends in Greenville nicely. Again, given the demographic, these were all white friends. My husband, Wayne, had a term he used when I would start to become close to a new friend. If a new friend called me on the phone and asked for me, Wayne would say, "It's your new best friend," as he handed me the phone. I do make friends easily. I think it is because I am easy to talk to and I am genuinely interested in the lives of others. Being an extrovert helps. Many of my friends see me as a problem solver; I can listen and offer suggestions for how they can deal with their dilemmas.

In February, 2010, I was on vacation in Trinidad celebrating the annual Carnival festival. Early one morning my computer started "pinging," notifying me that I had received some email. It turned out that I had received three emails from three dietitians/colleagues telling me that a management position in nutrition and food services at the hospital in Greenville– the one from which I had been fired - had come available, and that I only had a few days to get my application in. I read the job ad and the competencies they asked for and saw that I was well qualified for the position. I quickly contacted a few colleagues including my old vice president from Ultra Care, Dennis, a couple of directors still employed at the teaching hospital, the past CEO from Georgetown hospital, and a few others. They were all very encouraging and said they would be delighted to be references.

I thought this job would be a seamless transition, also fulfilling and challenging, and that it would energize me. So I submitted what I thought was a strong application. I didn't even receive an interview. I had been blocked again and not even given a chance to be interviewed. I wrote all my supporting colleagues that had been behind my application. I tried to be upbeat, saying I guess it wasn't my time, and thanked them for their support, but inside, I felt broken.

I sat down and wrote the following rap/poem: I felt better after I had completed it. Putting my feelings on paper has always been therapeutic.

Sticks and Stones (March 2010)
I understand and I accept
Sticks and stones may break my bones but words won't hurt me
Actions won't hurt me, either. My mantra:
I will rise above the fray

I understand
Edmonton 1969, a simple job, working a cash register,
I apply and I am told by a nice and polite man
I really want to give you a break but Black is bad for business
I think of my mantra, sticks and stones,
I am not broken, I will rise above the fray

An education is what I need to rise,
It is 1972, 2 years of night school and here I am at university
Hey Spook, go fetch, off the boat, all said in serious jest,
But these are words, they don't break my bones
I can rise above the fray
Its 1976, a nutrition degree in hand,
I will rise above the fray

To Montreal I head, many Blacks are there as well,
It is open, outspoken, a great place to go,
I have read Two Solitudes you know,
But it is the same, no political correctness here,
Nigger, jigaboo, I'm called, don't they know,
It isn't sticks or stones, only words I say,
I have risen above the fray

A year goes by, an internship finished,
Ontario is my favorite Province,
A first job in Madison, my bags are packed,
My Toronto friends say, Madison?
So conservative you know,

They have given me my first job,
They must be nice I say,
My education will help me
To rise above the fray.

Married in 1979, I'm off again to Franklin,
German town, is there prejudice, I wonder?
6 years later, a management degree part way,
But no promotions to be had
Sad, but not forlorn, Greenville beckons
My Toronto friends again say, Greenville?
It's so conservative you know,
They've given me my next job,
They must be nice I say,
I will rise above the fray

Two degrees in hand, I set out to make my way
Nice words and actions abound,
No sticks and stones are thrown my way
Hard work builds a great reputation
But here's a new manager, doesn't she know,
Her words and actions begin to break me
My mantra falters,
To be Canadian you must change!
I will fire you because you don't fit
You don't talk or act like me you know

Maybe three degrees will help?
I cannot change the way I look, the way I talk,
My personality is who I am
An education is what I need to rise above the fray
An MBA is the answer, everyone agrees
An MBA will help me rise above the fray

Three years more education, I return to Greenville town,
I obtain some great experiences
Hired to teach and mold great minds at university
Even President of our College is added to my repertoire

I bide my time for the ultimate job to be advertised
Its 12 years you know, since my MBA degree
Many of my colleagues call, have you seen? It's there,
Professional Practice Leader, I have all the qualifications,
I apply with gusto, every line, every word I check in my application
I wait, I wait, I do not understand,
Calls abound, have you been interviewed they ask?
I do not know what to say.
Sticks and stones,
But my mantra doesn't work,
Feeling broken; Education isn't the answer,
It will not help me to rise above the fray,

Education gave me a professional career,
Would I never break the glass ceiling?
As a black woman I know that I have to work
Twice as hard to get half as far.

As bad as not getting the job interview was, and as bad as things were at Cornerstone hospital, a worse nightmare began when my husband was diagnosed with prostate cancer. I had adapted to my manager's rules, but what she put me through while I was dealing with my husband's illness and subsequent death was more devastating, hurtful and demoralizing than I could have imagined.

It was September, 2009. My husband sat me down and said he had some news to share with me. He said that he had been diagnosed with prostate cancer and that he had had a biopsy that would tell him his prognosis. He explained that in early spring he had been diagnosed with an enlarged prostate and had been given a referral to do blood work. He went to the lab for his blood work but was told that because he had drunk some tea that morning the blood work could not be done. Of course the "nothing by mouth," or fasting restriction, is not typically required anymore for blood work, but it was at that time.

Wayne had waited five months before he finally did his blood work again. By this time he had additional symptoms. His results came back and they were not good; he had prostate cancer and his cancer had metastasized. I arranged to speak with his urologist. When I spoke with him I received the most distressing news, I had ever received: there was no treatment that could lead to a cure. Radiation and chemotherapy would be used but these would be more palliative than curative. They could buy him some time. I asked, "How long," and was told that Wayne had about a year and a half. I burst out crying and I don't think I stopped crying for many years.

The first six months of Wayne's illness were actually fairly normal in terms of our routine. My life was still very busy between teaching at the University two evenings a week, my full time job at Cornerstone hospital, preparing meals for the family and all the other responsibilities of being a mother to three sons.

One of my sons was still a teenager in his last year of high school. I did spend happy moments with Wayne at my son's football games. My son enjoyed competitive sports and had won many awards. Wayne loved going to his high school football games. My son was recruited by Sir Wilfrid Laurier University in Kitchener, Ontario. As Wayne's illness progressed, my son became more distraught and he eventually dropped out from university in Kitchener to return home to be with his father. If he had attended university closer to home, he might have stayed at university. As it was, he dropped out and never went back to university. My other two sons were both in their mid- to late twenties, and both were unsettled.

The fall was Wayne's busiest time. He ran his own business, Alexander Pools, which he ran with our oldest son. In the winter, Wayne was also the director of the snow school at The Slopes in Greenville. Against his doctor's advice, Wayne skied his heart out that winter of 2009-10. His cancer had metastasized to his bones and a break would probably not heal, but he skied anyway. I'm sure at some level Wayne knew this was his last season doing something he loved.

It was in the spring of 2010 that events took a turn for the worse. The pain became unbearable; he could not pee and had to be catheterized. He would double up in pain as he passed sediment through his catheter. If you've ever had kidney stones you can understand how much pain he experienced. But Wayne did not complain.

My stress was beginning to get out of control as I tried to continue to run my life. I realized that I needed support from Cornerstone hospital to be able to deal with the situation. I expected, given the gravity of the circumstances I was going through, that my employer would understand my need to flex my starting and ending time. I was wrong. I contacted my manager Lena and told her what was happening. Her first response was to question whether or not I was telling her the truth. My manager Lena's rationale was that in her experience no one died of prostate cancer anymore; many people died with it but not because of it. I had already told her that Wayne's cancer had metastasized but this didn't change her response; she would not give me any flex time.

I suffered in silence. Wayne continued to work in an administrative capacity at The Slopes that winter of 2010-11. And since he held a senior position at the club, he was the person who was interviewed by the local TV channel in November 2010. They did a small clip of him smiling and discussing the great early ski conditions that the ski club was experiencing. No one could have known in that interview that Wayne was wearing a concealed catheter. The next day at work at Cornerstone hospital, everyone whom I met in my department and my manager made a point of telling me that they saw the newscast from the night before. I was told that: "You have obviously exaggerated your situation. How could you ask for flexibility in your hours?"

The favor I had asked for was to be able to flex my time to be able to deal with the kinds of situations that are bound to arise when living with a person with a terminal illness. I wasn't asking to work less than eight hours. If Wayne was having a bad morning I wanted to go into work at nine instead of eight thirty. If he had a late afternoon doctor's appointment I wanted to come to work earlier in the morning, at seven thirty instead of eight thirty. She refused my request and said I was asking for special treatment. Her reasoning was that if she granted me this favor then she would be opening the gates for all kinds of requests for flexibility. I thought to myself that I would have hoped that she would show more compassion to me or others in a similar situation. Obviously not.

I remember one morning very clearly. Wayne just wanted to talk to me because he was having a bad morning. I looked at the time and had to stop him mid-sentence because if he finished sharing, I would not make it to work on time. If I punched in at even 8:35, five minutes late, it would be recorded as a late on my timecard. I stopped Wayne mid-sentence and said I would call from the car. It took me another ten minutes of driving to compose myself and call. I could not let him hear my voice breaking and the distress I felt.

In the mornings, before I would leave for work, I assessed his condition. Did he have problems with his bowels? Did he have pain? Did he need a rub down, which relaxed him when he was in pain? Some mornings he did, some mornings he did not. Did he have any appointments that afternoon that I could attend with him?

In the winter of 2010-11, I was a full-time clinical dietitian. My work hours were 8:30 am - 4:30 pm. I would come into work and review the consult sheets with patient information, diagnoses, new admissions and discharges. From these sheets I would plan my day and decide which patients were a priority. Most days I would complete my consultations by late afternoon, at which time I would complete my charting, emails, and deskwork. In most hospitals clinical dietitians worked flexible hours but at Cornerstone hospital we were unionized, and we had to have set hours.

Although Wayne's urologist had done the diagnosis, the doctor overseeing his chemotherapy was managing his treatment. She in turn referred him to a radiologist for radiation to relieve his pain. They were supposed to start chemotherapy but had delayed it, He was, instead, treated with repeated doses of radiation. At that same time Wayne began to retain fluid in his lower extremities. His feet became so swollen he could hardly walk. I kept saying that I didn't think this was being caused by the cancer in his bones. I pleaded with Wayne to set up a consult with the doctor managing his treatment.

As a result of that consult, an X-ray of Wayne's lower bowel was ordered. As soon as they saw the X-ray an ambulance was called. Wayne had to be rushed to the hospital because he had a ruptured intestine. The repeated radiation had thinned his bowel to the point where it had ruptured. He had been bleeding internally for some time and this is what had been causing the pain and edema (fluid retention). He was admitted for emergency surgery. I left work and met the ambulance at emergency. I spent a harrowing night at the hospital but thankfully Wayne survived the surgery. I hadn't slept all night so I called in sick the next day.

At this time as you can imagine I was not sleeping well at nights. Often I would just cry uncontrollably, and I was losing weight. I went to see the staff nurse at Cornerstone to be able to talk to someone and maybe get some advice. The nurse was very sympathetic and thought I should take some time off. If only my manager felt the same way!

Wayne was in the hospital for a few days after his operation. A couple of days after my return to work after the operation, I received a notice from my manager that she was giving me a written warning about being off sick. I knew the process involved in attendance management programs. After three absences, whatever the reason, you would be disciplined and could be fired. According to my manager, this was my second absence.

After work I spent my evenings at the hospital with Wayne. Because of how thin his skin was, his incision had been stapled but it was not completely closed because his skin couldn't be stretched that far.

I continued to work and be on time; I couldn't have any more attendance incidents. I still taught my two courses at the university, but was able to delegate some of that work to my teaching assistants. I also developed a matrix which enabled me to delegate the marking of my student assignments to a couple of registered dietitian colleagues. In June, I had completed my last term at the College of Dietitians, so I no longer had any commitments there.

My condition was becoming noticeable. I would burst out crying uncontrollably when I thought of my circumstances. I tried to hide the spontaneous tears but my whole demeanor had changed. I am usually a happy person, confident in my abilities and someone who laughs a lot.

Despite my husband's illness and in spite of my treatment by management at Cornerstone hospital, my work was rewarding and satisfying. I could still enjoy my job. But my change in appearance and attitude were becoming more obvious than I thought. A few nurse colleagues steered me into a conference room and asked me what was going on. I shared my story with them. They told me that I needed to be away for a while and perhaps get some counseling. They also suggested I should go to the vice president of nursing. They thought she would understand because her husband had had a heart attack and she was granted a month off with pay while she nursed him back to health.

I was encouraged by this advice and set up an appointment with the VP of nursing. I told her what I was going through and that I wanted to go on a short-term sick leave. She had, however, been speaking to my manager. She said that she had heard that I was asking for "special treatment" and that instead of sick leave I could take a leave of absence without pay to look after my husband and at the end of that leave she would reconsider my return to work. I sat there in shock. I could not take an unpaid leave of absence because my medical benefits would end. There was obviously no sympathy from her. She had her administrative assistant escort me out of her office.

To this day when I look back on what happened, I find it hard to believe that they saw me in such a stereotypical way. Did they see me only as a Black woman who had gotten all these benefits from immigrating to Canada; did they see me only as an immigrant who was taking advantage of the situation, instead of just being grateful for what I had?

I decided to visit the staff nurse again; she was the one who had suggested that in her assessment I should go off on sick leave or short-term disability. I had thought that perhaps I could get some formal recommendation to be able to go on sick leave. Unfortunately, she had some bad news for me. She informed me that the only way I could get to go on sick leave or short-term disability was if a psychiatrist had diagnosed me as depressed.

You did not have to be in health care to know that a referral to a psychiatrist would take months. I realized I had to continue working. I thought that although I was stressed I could still do my work effectively. It was only a few days later that this assumption proved to be wrong. I was completing an intensive care assessment. My routine was to explain my assessment to the nurse looking after the patient. I checked with the ward clerk who told me that the nurse I needed to speak with was Sally, and that she was at bed 3. I then asked the ward clerk, "Sally? Is she new?" The ward clerk looked at me as if I was from Mars and said, "Cecily, you know Sally!"

Of course I knew Sally! She and I had started at Cornerstone hospital together and we had had our orientation together, twelve years ago. She was my "go to" nurse, the one I went to with any patient concerns.

I realized I wasn't thinking as clearly as I had thought I was. I probably couldn't trust myself to be able to assess my patients clearly. In intensive care I often had a patient's life in my hands. A mistake in an assessment could put a patient at risk. I would never do that, whatever the consequences. I left the hospital that day. It was just about midday. I got my handbag and briefcase and walked to my car.

I do not know how I drove from the hospital to my doctor's office. I said to his receptionist that I needed to see him. She took one look at my obvious distress and asked me to sit down. I was ushered in next. My doctor listened to my story. He said he was shocked, and that what the health nurse and upper management had said to me was unethical. He said there was no law saying that I had to be diagnosed by a psychiatrist. He diagnosed me as depressed with a situational depression. He said he signed the papers for patients going on stress leave all the time.

This made me feel so sad. How could my employer be so cruel? Did they not have any empathy? They were health care workers. They were in health care because at some point they wanted to help make sick people better. How could they not see me as a person in need of some compassion? I know now that my manager's behaviour wasn't only budget-related it was personal. I had been at Cornerstone hospital for over 12 years. Why, in my time of need, didn't this count for something? I took the papers my doctor had signed for me, took them back to the hospital and was granted sick leave from Cornerstone.

Wayne began to go downhill quickly after this. The day that he was supposed to be released, I went to get him dressed and I saw that his pajamas were soaked in blood. His sutures had separated. If this had happened minutes later, after the discharge, he would have lost his bed. Instead he was booked for immediate follow-up surgery. In this surgery, in addition to suturing him again, they had to do a colostomy. Wayne was devastated, although they said that it was probably only temporary. After the surgery he returned home. A home care provider came in daily to change his dressings and an aide came in to give him baths and change his colostomy. As much as these home care providers told me that these were their responsibilities, I would often bath him and change his colostomy myself.

We had another dilemma; Wayne's surgeries delayed his chemotherapy. The surgical team insisted that his body would not withstand chemotherapy for at least a couple months, but because we had already waited so long the cancer had now metastasized to his liver. I knew from my patients how liver failure would lead inevitably to jaundice, weight loss and a painful death. I thought that Wayne really needed palliative chemotherapy to perhaps buy him some additional time.

We went to see his doctor to discuss chemotherapy. She could not believe how much he had deteriorated in one month. She said that it was too soon for chemotherapy. The chances were thirty percent that it would be successful and seventy percent that he would die. Not good odds. The other option was not to do chemotherapy. But then he would progress into liver failure; he would live a few more months, but he would have a painful, debilitating death. Together we made the decision to take the poor odds of thirty percent. He was admitted to the chemotherapy ward. The doctor there was not pleased at this admission - he knew the odds. I told him that we also knew and had discussed them with our doctor and that we would take those odds. Yes, we were hoping for a miracle. I emphasized that all decisions should go through me as I had the medical background and Wayne trusted my judgment.

To my surprise - or maybe not - the physician said to me, "Be his wife, not his clinician." It may have sounded like good advice, but to me at the time I thought he was being patronizing. I returned to Wayne's room to find him surrounded by medical interns. The physician-in-charge was talking to Wayne. The physician-in-charge asked me to leave the room; Wayne was competent to make his own decisions and this being the case, I could not make decisions for him.

During my entire career, I had stood up to doctors like this, so I spoke directly to Wayne and said, "Wayne can you tell the doctor that I can make your medical decisions for you." Wayne reinforced that we had discussed this and that all decisions should be run by me. Throughout his illness Wayne refused to acknowledge his pain, and had refused most of his pain meds. I spent every day in the hospital with him, just leaving for an hour when I went home for a quick bath and change of clothes. When I was unable to be with him, our sons or good friends of ours would come and sit with him. When I was with him, I would climb into the single bed and try to find a space between all the IV and other lines for us to cuddle as we did at home for thirty-two years, or thirty-eight if I count the time before we got married.

This time was trying for me. I knew too much. I remember when Wayne was put on TPN (total parenteral nutrition) where he would be fed through a central vein as he couldn't be fed by a tube feeding into his digestive track. They started his TPN but did not decrease his IV line. Wayne was therefore receiving double his fluid needs. I witnessed his limbs swelling before my eyes. No doctors were present as it was after hours and the residents that were present wouldn't make the decision to decrease his IV line without the specialist permission. You can understand that I thought many times that I should decrease his IV myself, but the reason I didn't was that the doctor and staff would know it was me who did this and I was sure I would be banned from being in his room altogether.

I cried that night for everything: losing my husband, my children losing their dad, my job situation, my life. My expertise was nutrition support and I couldn't apply my knowledge when it was needed most. Wayne's deterioration was rapid after this. A few days later they discontinued his TPN. They said they would transfer him to palliative care when a bed became available. The last travesty happened the night his TPN was discontinued, when they transferred him from his single room to a double room, I pleaded with them not to move him and offered to pay whatever was needed to keep the private room. The next day Wayne passed away with all of his family around him. I wasn't there. I had just slipped out for three minutes to take a phone call. I clung on to the belief that loved ones wait for their closest loved one to leave their presence, giving then permission to transition to their next life.

Wayne was only sixty-three years old, a life left too soon. We had just begun planning our retirement. We were going to travel and just do the things we loved to do together.

But it wasn't meant to be. He had lived for one and a half years after his diagnosis. Exactly the length of time his urologist had predicted. A counsellor I saw after Wayne's death called cancer "a blessing that sucks." The blessing is that we had eighteen months together after his diagnosis, to say how much we loved each other and for Wayne to receive as many back, feet, forehead and even eyeball rubs as he desired. He loved massages. If I went away for a few days he would count the days I was away and get double rubs for the next few days to make up. Our love for each other was strong to the end. I had found my perfect soulmate and had lost him before we had a chance to grow old together.

One of the things that kept me going during the last months of Wayne's illness was the love and support of our friends. I had the unbearable situation in my workplace but in the evenings, I had the love of our many friends. I was introduced to a web site called Caringbridge.org. This is a site where you can do a daily blog and friends can join the blog and write their comments. There were hundreds of loving comments from our friends and Wayne's colleagues. Every evening I would read the day's entries to Wayne. We really felt the love. This was reinforced at his funeral. I reserved the Anglican Cathedral in Greenville and every seat was filled, over seven hundred people. Our family was very moved.

One of the joys that Wayne introduced into my life, was skiing. It was his love also. He taught me to ski in 1973. In 1974, after Wayne graduated from university, we headed to Banff, Alberta, with another couple in an old station wagon, with a mattress in the back to sleep on. I had driven out to Banff in the summer of 1973 and was moved by the beauty of the drive. This winter drive was different but just as scenic, especially the snow-covered spruce and fir trees; they sparkled and twinkled in the morning sunlight, welcoming us. There, we met eight other ski instructors who were good friends. After a hard day of skiing, the guys would head to the bar for a few pints. Before they left I would collect one dollar from everyone and with ten dollars I would cook a hot meal on a two burner stove in our little motel. At six sharp we would eat supper and then head to bed so we could be up early to hit the slopes and make the first run. We skied at Sunshine, Mount Norquay and Lake Louise. I was hooked for life; a real joy.

After that introduction, we skied every winter and would end the season with a special trip, with family and friends. When our children were young, we would head to the Eastern Townships in Quebec or to closer hills in the United States, like Alpine Valley, Boyne Mountain or Ellicottville. Our biggest family trips were to Big White and Whistler in British Columbia.

When the children were older, I started planning ski trips with my girlfriends. Our group for the past ten years is the SSS (Sexy Ski Sisters). I love my "sistas" as we call each other. We have chosen Utah as our "go to" place for the past five years. We ski at Powder

Mountain. This mountain has 8,000 acres of pristine terrain in the Wasatch Mountains. As they only sell 1500 tickets, they never have lineups. You can be alone on the top of this vastness, looking onto the beauty of it all. It is a remarkable hidden treasure, not pretentious as many ski resorts can be. There aren't any fancy ski shops with expensive gear. Even the cost of food in their restaurant and cafeteria is very reasonable. The slopes are never as crowded because Powder Mountain limits the number of daily skiers. We then head to our condos after a full day of skiing. Two sistas get together each evening to cook a gourmet meal for the group of ten. After supper we chat over wine into the late evening.

My sistas come from all over Canada: Four different cities in Ontario, Nova Scotia, and British Columbia. I love these evenings, the warmth and camaraderie is palpable. We can't stop hugging each other and telling each other how we look forward to this week every year.

My Sistas (the SSS)

My short-term disability leave at Cornerstone hospital was coming to an end, but I still wasn't feeling well enough to go back to work. I was still crying spontaneously and feeling lethargic. Then one of my close friends contacted me. She worked in Africa for a Norwegian aid group. Her project at that time was called "Kicking AIDS Out," which was empowering young girls through sport. She asked me to travel with her. We visited Zambia,

Botswana and Zimbabwe. My doctor had already agreed that I still wasn't ready to return to work so I went with my friend to Africa after my short-term disability ended.

That trip provided the healing that I needed. Africa was beautiful. I had never seen sunsets so orange; they covered the whole sky. I was familiar with Trinidad and Tobago sunsets that lasted only minutes. In Africa the sunsets last much longer. The open landscape was covered with the sparkle of it all. I really think that I started to heal on these evenings when I would sit quietly and just stare into the evening sky. There was also a big star that I looked for every night. I envisioned Wayne in that shining star. He was the love of my life, connecting with me at the other side of the world.

My journey to Africa was a wonderful experience: safaris, interesting villages and beautiful sunsets. I wondered, given my ancestry, if I would feel a sense of belonging in Africa. After all, a few hundred years ago I had ancestors from this continent. I liked everyone I met. But no, I didn't feel that connection to the people or the place. It didn't feel like my lost home. Africans accepted me immediately as half-African, they called me "Mukeda" in Zimbabwean meaning, I was Black like them, but I was still someone "from away."

It was on this trip to Africa that I knew in my heart who I was. I was first, a Trinidadian, and second, a Canadian; I was a Trinidad-Canadian. When I return to Trinidad on vacation I get a happy feeling, I laugh more and chat more, I can be totally myself. However, I feel the same way when my vacation is over. I am glad to be back in Canada. Why do Canadians want you to give up half of who you are to prove that you are Canadian? I say to anyone who will listen, don't be so concerned about immigrants not being Canadian enough. It only takes one generation. My children, as first generation offspring, think they are one hundred percent Canadian. They know that I am from Trinidad and they love to come to Trinidad on vacation and go to the beach and visit family, but they know that they are Canadians visiting their mother's homeland.

After returning from Africa at the beginning of June, 2011, I felt strong enough to face returning to work. My plans were to work for 6 months and then retire from Cornerstone hospital in November of that year. I plunged into work and was happy to reconnect with colleagues that I hadn't seen for the past three months.

Nothing had changed. I had been back at work for two weeks when my manager, Lena, made an appointment to see me. She gave me my third formal disciplinary action for a sick time incident and asked me a series of questions from a form she was filling out. Then she got to the main question: "What was I going to do to prevent this absence from happening again?" I looked at her in disbelief and said, "I will hope that none of my sons die or get a terminal illness." I asked, "Why are you doing this?" She said she was just following the rules!

I should mention here that until my husband became ill, I had had perfect attendance at this job and I'd had perfect attendance in all my previous jobs. Some days I might not have felt well, but I would always make it into work. So my manager's pretense of disciplining me for poor attendance was particularly ironic. You should realize that my three absences occurred over the period of one year, during the most critical stage of my husband's illness. I didn't have time to explore and understand my hospital's attendance management policy. All I understood from my manager was that there were three meetings with her and after three strikes I could be fired after the fourth incident.

This is what I was led to believe.

For this memoir I have researched attendance management. I realize that one of the categories of attendance management is called "non-culpable absenteeism," which occurs when an employee, through no fault of their own, is absent from work due to legitimate illness or injury. Non-culpable absenteeism is managed in a non-disciplinary manner, with the intent of providing assistance to the employee to attend work regularly. Although this was my husband's illness, my absences were non-culpable. I should have been offered counseling, instead of being written up and threatened with termination.

When I gave my manager my retirement papers a month later, she chastised me for not telling her that I had planned to retire when she was giving me my third absence warning. She said if she had known then it would not have been necessary. I just looked at her blankly and felt numb. The microaggressions against me were going to end; there was a date; I would be leaving in three months. I could focus on the future. I was about to retire from hospital dietetics after thirty-three years.

I actually enjoyed my last three months at Cornerstone hospital. I was able to say goodbye to some of my colleagues. I continued to take long walks all over Ashford with one of my new friends, a social worker who was new at the hospital. They had a nice farewell party for me which was attended by some of the upper management team, in addition to many nurses and the health care professionals I worked with on a daily basis. All three of my sons attended for support and for that I was very grateful.

Chapter 14

Retirement from Hospital & Clinical Dietetics, 2011 - Present

After retiring from Cornerstone hospital, I still continued to teach at the university until 2013 and to run an independent practicum internship program. I have worked in all areas of dietetics over the years and running my independent internship program has been very fulfilling professional work. Mentoring bright, ambitious, and motivated interns has been a joy to me. I thrive on their success at the end of their journey. These interns need someone like me to champion their journey. My reward is their success, their appreciation for my mentorship and for helping them become the professionals they aspire to be. Every year, when I decide to finally hang up my hat, there is one more student asking me to take her on with her plea that there is nowhere else for them to do their practicum. I know only too well that they are probably correct in this assessment and have most often made the decision to take on another student.

Carrying on after the death of a spouse at a relatively young age has not been easy. I had three adult sons to support in their grief and, as we all know, everyone grieves differently. One thing we had in common was that we were all close to tears in the months following Wayne's death. My sons loved their father. I also knew how much they loved me by the many ways they tried to comfort me. I still had trouble sleeping despite taking a nightly sleeping pill. My middle son would lie next to me and recite relaxation exercises over and over until I dozed off. I cried every day for over a year. Even when someone said something funny about Wayne the tears would appear.

Then a good friend gave me a book called *I Can't Stop Crying*, by Martin and Ferris. It gave me some comfort, not in stopping the tears, but in understanding why. Everyone stops grieving in their own time. A year and a half after Wayne's death, in September of 2012, I held a memorial for Wayne at the ski club where he worked. We held it near a tree into which the club had carved a caricature of his face, just below a ski run they had named after him, called "Wayne's Way." I took a bottle of Trinidadian rum that Wayne would have loved and everyone had a shot and reminisced. I think that was the moment I thought of moving on.

Later that fall a Trinidad couple invited me to go on a Caribbean cruise with them. A group of about sixty Trinidadians from a Toronto-based club had organized the cruise. I played with the thought that I might meet a nice Trinidadian on this trip. Unfortunately, this did not happen. Oh I had a couple passes; one fellow told me he was single only to find out that his girlfriend was on the cruise with him! Another was from a man who I found out was already married but that his wife wasn't on the cruise with him. These interactions were not about discovering similar interests like art, theatre, music, travel. They were all about sex; not even intimacy, but sex.

I was so discouraged. This experience ended my desire to meet someone from Trinidad. Many of my single friends were online dating, but I just couldn't imagine using the Internet as a way of meeting a potential partner myself. What scared me most was the 40 years or so of someone else's life that I would have to learn about. When I met Wayne in my twenties, we only had to catch up on the few years when we moved away from our parents' homes. Online dating seemed too intimidating, so I gave up on the idea. I had a big group of girlfriends with whom I travelled and did other things with. I had my three sons and my brother and his two daughters and their five girls, my great nieces. Maybe I didn't really need a male partner? I honestly thought that there were so many people I loved platonically. I reasoned that spending time and continuing to develop these platonic relationships would be fulfilling enough.

At the end of the year I was invited to a staff reunion at my Ultra Care hospital - yes, the same hospital from which I had been fired - but I had had so many good friends when I worked there, and most of us were either retired or about to, so I went. It was a wonderful event, catching up with old colleagues and finding out where their paths had taken them after they had left the hospital. At the end of the evening I made it over to chat with an old friend, Jan. He had been the medical librarian at the hospital and a past manager who had started a year after I did in 1986.

In chatting, I said that I had been to five weddings of my students that year and I missed having someone to dance with. Jan had dated a dear girlfriend of mine while we were both working at the hospital, so I knew he was a great dancer; would he like to be my guest at the next wedding? He said he would love to. A couple weeks later Jan called to ask me. "Cecily, did you mean getting together as friends or romantically?" I said, "We'll see." It was at this time that I began to consider romantic love. I reasoned that with a new partner I would need more than romance. I would need someone to really understand me, I needed a spiritual connection. I was protective of my soul. My faith in humanity had been affected in my past work environments, I wasn't willing to let anyone into my personal life who I thought was disingenuous.

We did get together romantically in 2013 and have been together ever since. I love the fact that Jan is so different from Wayne. Wayne and I loved the outdoors, skiing, spending time in the country at the farm, travelling and getting together with our many groups of friends. Jan, on the other hand, plays guitar and harmonica, he sings and had been in a number of local bands. He is a poet, with three books published; he loves the theater, art, and is an avid reader, including many of the books about the Caribbean, race and ethnicity. We discuss the world and politics together and hold similar views.

I cannot believe that I am so lucky to have found love twice in my life. Jan is so creative and has opened up my love for jazz and the blues. We spend our free time following the live music scene. Jan is often invited to play his harmonica with some of the *artistes* in Greenville. The parties that I attend with him are music-oriented and folks arrive with their instruments; some time that evening they will usually break out in song. A funny occurrence that has happened more than once is that I would be invited to join Jan in singing when he is performing. The assumption that all Blacks can not only sing but sing well is a stereotype. When I decline, I usually say, "Not all Blacks can sing, but I can dance," with a smile on my face. Our spare time is spent visiting museums and art galleries in Ontario and across the border in Detroit and Buffalo. We are active theatre goers locally as well as at the Shaw Festival in Niagara-on-the-Lake and the Stratford Festival. He describes himself as a feminist, meaning he supports women's rights to equality in society and the workplace. For this reason he is one of my few white friends that can truly empathize with my struggles in the workplace.

He has also made a great travel partner and we have made many international trips together. We have visited Iceland, Spain, Portugal, Malta, Morocco, New Orleans and his parent's homeland, Poland, in addition to our yearly trips to my first home, Trinidad and Tobago. Neither of us wants to remarry and we live in our separate homes. We are in a committed, long-term relationship but choose to live apart. Our situation is apparently not uncommon at our age. There is even an acronym that describes us: LATs, Living Apart Together. Jan is a white, first-generation

Polish-Canadian, so he has experienced a bit of the prejudice that comes from growing up Polish in a predominantly WASP culture in Ottawa in the 1960's. Both his parents are dead and he readily agrees with my assessment that they would have had a hard time back then accepting the fact that he was dating a woman of color. Thankfully, Jan has no such concerns, and we are happy together.

I have the time now to explore my creative side, my right hemisphere. My academic life has been for the most part, a left brain activity. Some of my new creative experiences include painting. Sitting for hours quietly making a scene come to life is a meditative, peaceful experience. Writing is also a creative activity, this memoir is my second book since retirement.

Meech Lake, my first painting

Tobago Beach (my happy place)

Wayne's death was hard on the whole family. My oldest son took over Alexander Pools. He struggled at first being an owner, hiring staff, doing the books, scheduling his appointments and taking over all of the technical parts of the job. After a long learning curve I can happily say that he is handling things well. My middle son has an entrepreneurial spirit and I decided to help him to express this. After a few unsuccessful ventures, he has found his niche and has turned out to be the most financially successful yet. I also admire his role as a father to his son, my oldest grandson. My son is a loving father and involved in my grandson's life.

My youngest son did not return to university and, after being unsettled for a while, entered into a trade apprenticeship program. He is married and has a beautiful wife and two precious children. I knew he would be the first to be married. As a child he would preface many sentences with, "When I am a dad." I always knew this came from the fact that he had such a great example. He hasn't had any incidents with racism. I think this partly stems from the fact that I call him my white child, he definitely "can pass" as we say in Trinidad. Wayne would joke that my genes got weaker with each kid, referring of course to the color of their skin.

The next picture shows how much my three boys vary in color.

Immigration, Race and Survival

I travel to the U.S. about three times a year. Some of these visits are to see my brother, his two daughters, and my five beautiful great-nieces. I have occasionally gone by plane but mostly by car. My travel companions have usually been my white girlfriends. Although I am a law-abiding visitor, I am also very aware of American police and I do admit that I am scared of them. My first encounter that alerted me to be more aware was a trip to the Pocono Mountains. I was traveling with a white girlfriend and we were joining my sister-in-law for her birthday get-together with her two daughters. This was over twenty years ago, so we did not have any digital devices, just paper maps. It was nighttime, dark in the mountains and we couldn't find our exit. We had driven up and down the main road a few times looking for our turnoff. We pulled into a deserted parking lot to look at our maps again.

My friend alerted me to a police car pulling in behind us. I thought, "Great! Finally some help." To my surprise the policeman said that he and his partner had observed us driving by a few times. He shone his flashlight in my face and demanded to know what we were doing in the area. He hadn't come to help, but to interrogate me. I realized that he saw a black face and was suspicious. My explanations seemed to satisfy the policeman because he let us go without further harassment. I have since come to characterize this all too common phenomenon as the police needing an explanation for why I was "driving while Black."

My second encounter with a policeman and "driving while Black" was just a couple of years ago in Michigan. I was driving with my daughter-in-law and my two grandchildren on our way to Florida. The Interstate was closed and all traffic was being detoured to a single lane by-pass. I put my blinker on and merged into the by-pass lane when I was "bumped" in my rear by a transport truck, which had not seen me merging in time to slow down. We pulled off the road. He jumped out of his truck, very apologetic, and asked if we were okay. I said we were. My rear bumper was slightly damaged but his truck had no damage whatsoever.

In a matter of minutes, however, before we could decide our next steps, a white policeman arrived along with a white bystander. The bystander had called the police on his cell. He began shouting that he had seen it all, that it was my fault and that I should be charged and that he would be willing to come to court as a witness. I started to tell the policeman what had happened, and the policeman looked at me and said, "Shut up!" I was shocked and I walked away, composing myself.

Now, I admit, my example is not as overt as the Amy Cooper incident where a Black man suggested that she obey the posted signs to leash her dog in Central Park in New York. Amy responded with all the white privilege she knew she had. She called the police and said that an African American man was threatening her and to send the cops immediately. Why did she choose to lie? Was it because a Black man told her, a white woman, to follow the rules? It is obvious that she assumed that a white woman would be believed over a Black man. She knew that her race would give her an advantage and she could exploit the fears of Black men being a threat to white women. She thought that no one would accuse a white woman of playing the race card; that was something Blacks did, not whites. Thank goodness that Christian Cooper had the foresight to record the whole event.

In my case, the policeman chose to listen to a white bystander's version of events over mine and told me, a Black woman, to shut up. The bystander's version of events was immediately accepted as more credible. The policeman didn't even want to hear what I had to say and to listen to my side of the story. The bystander was exhibiting "white privilege" as he had called the cops and was confident that his version of events would be believed over mine. He was willing to present his version in court as he was confident of this fact.

I sat on the bumper of my car and began to assess my situation. At times like this, in order to decide on my next move, I use emotional intelligence self-awareness techniques. I quickly realized that I had to take back control. I walked over and said to the policeman that I had decided that I would fix my own car. The transport truck had incurred no damages so we wouldn't need to file an accident report. The bystander was still talking, repeating what he had said earlier. I looked at the truck driver who was looking very relieved. The policeman confirmed that the truck driver was okay with my decision and we all went on our way.

I haven't been in a work environment now for over nine years. I will not willingly put myself in a situation where my race is an issue. What many people do not realize is that when they make statements referring to "those immigrants", or "those refugees," they are also referring to me. I am successful in Canada partly because I came from a privileged, middle-class background. I came to Canada with sufficient funds to enable me to support myself through university and live in Montreal for a year without a stipend or job so I could do my internship. I recognize also that in the Caribbean and other developing countries, I am part of the "brain drain." I was the type of immigrant that Canada wanted, and which it continues to accept in increasing numbers. I still think, however, that many white Canadians do not fully appreciate the need for Canada to continue to accept immigrants in order to keep this country financially viable and culturally rich.

Canadians do not necessarily understand immigrants' contributions. Instead, they blame immigrants for their own problems, such as lack of jobs, increased crime, unavailable housing and economic shifts. An extensive education initiative needs to be established to change this mindset.

I will share an incident that occurred just over a year ago that illustrates my point. I was staying at a U.S. hotel with my white girlfriend, her husband and my white partner. I have known this girlfriend for 35 years. On our way to meet this couple for breakfast, my partner and I were in the elevator with a white American man whose T-shirt had a large American flag on it along with the words: *If this shirt offends you, pack your shit and find a new country to cry in.* Recognizing the t-shirt as likely being worn by a white supremacist, my partner and I quickly exited the elevator and made it over to the table our friends had secured.

In discussing the T-shirt, my girlfriend said that she did agree with some aspects of what the T-shirt implied and added that it applied to Canada also. When I pointed out that his t-shirt was offensive and anti-immigrant, she proceeded to itemize the reasons she agreed with the t-shirt's sentiment. Her reasons included Syrian conflict refugees who were "ungrateful" about having been granted asylum in Canada because they complained about a lack of affordable housing. Her reasons also included immigrants who felt entitled to try to steal from insurance companies by using a particular car scam that her law firm had to deal with on a chronic basis. Her reasons ended with a comment I have heard before, "Why can't they be more Canadian; why can't they be more like us."

Meaning: more "white." I have talked in an earlier chapter about the contributions immigrants make to the culture of Canada, making it more diverse and vibrant, and that succeeding generations are almost always more integrated than their parents. Gratefulness and entitlement are, of course, trigger words for fiscally conservative, anti-immigration advocates to use against non-white immigrants. If the Canadian government has said they will take in conflict refugees, and then doesn't provide a means to house them, hearing an immigrant complain about it doesn't mean they aren't grateful for Canada having given them asylum. It means they need a roof over their heads in order to survive with dignity. Just because a few insurance companies have to hire lawyers to deal with insurance fraud doesn't mean that immigrants as a whole feel entitled or don't have a good work ethic. In fact the literature is quite clear: most immigrants work very hard, often at lower-paying jobs, in order to provide security for their family and a better way of life for their children.

Unfortunately, my friend and I were not making any headway, so we dropped the discussion. Her response did make me sad, but I am still glad we had the discussion, and hope I may have moved her a little bit forward in awareness.

I also want to share with you how someone very close to me reacted when I told them that I was writing my memoir and that race would be a main theme of my book. His response was, "You are wrong to complain about racism. It's bullshit! You had no racism from your husband. You get no racism from your friends, 90% of whom are white. So you experienced some minor racist incidents in Edmonton and Montreal, and maybe some other insolence here or there. I have personally experienced worse than you, but I will not give power to racism by talking about it. What someone else thinks about me has no power over me. You give power to the minority of fools by making a mountain out of a mole hill. Rather than focusing on how Canada welcomed you with open arms and is your happy home, you focus on these isolated incidents in your life.

You are wrong and that makes me very sad."

Of course this rant is inaccurate in many ways, but I think it is useful to explore those inaccuracies. First off, I have not "complained." I have recounted incidents in my life and talked about how they made me feel and how I have come to interpret them in their implications. Second, I don't "give power to racism" by talking about it. Although I got fired or was blocked from certain opportunities because of my color, I moved on in spite of my experiences. It remains important to me to continue to call out actions when Blacks are not treated equally and fairly.

My friend is correct in one respect, however: the majority of my friends are white, as demonstrated by the picture in my back yard below of my party to celebrate my fiftieth year in Canada. We had a group shot, and yes, most of my friends are white.

Celebrating my 50th year in Canada in 2019 with my friends; happy times (All dressed in Canada flag colors)

Writing my memoir has also made me reflect on why I haven't been the recipient of more overt and covert prejudice. One main reason has been the fact that my husband was white. I was accepted by his friends as his wife and partner. When I am traveling with my husband and present partner, who is also white, and my white girlfriends, I cross borders without any questions. I realize now that I have benefited from their "white privilege." As soon as I am by myself or with another person of colour I am treated differently. As recently as a couple years ago I was visiting my American family for an after-Christmas visit with my cousin and her son. Again, we were hauled into immigration. I looked around at the group who were waiting to be interrogated. There was not one white face among the group. After waiting an hour, standing up as there were no free seats, we were finally seen by a customs officer, who just stamped our passports and sent us on our way.

I couldn't write a book on prejudice without examining my own. I have re-examined my concept of prejudice. Some of the most common, pervasive types of prejudice include racism, sexism, ageism, classism, nationalism, religion or xenophobia. When I examine this list and I look at my nineteen years in Trinidad, classism was undoubtedly one of the prejudices I held then. Racism, in the form of color prejudice was also present, but as I related earlier, in 1973, while writing a university paper where I looked at class and color, my conclusion was that class trumped color in Trinidad. There were Black - not colored - members of my parents' family circle. Prior Jones, a Black friend of my father comes to mind. He played cricket with my father and they were friends long after their cricket days and I called him uncle. There wasn't a distinction with the many successful Blacks in Trinidad with whom my family socialized. There was a distinction with the poorer Blacks, and my family definitely demonstrated classist behavior.

In examining my prejudices today I have asked myself the question, who do I dislike? My great-aunt talked about vulgar, common people, individuals who were coarse or rude, quick to use foul language. I have come across people like this, and I tend to do anything to get out of their path and not engage with them; I avoid them at all costs. In analyzing my prejudices, I realize that I also dislike vulgar people. I realize, as well, that it is easy to make the assumption that this is still classist. The stereotype around crude or vulgar behavior is that this is a trait of the poor or uneducated. I don't believe, however, that my prejudice is purely classist. I do not stereotype poor and uneducated people as all being crude and vulgar; in fact I have found a number of wealthy, educated people whom I consider to be crude and vulgar.

Because I have experienced racism and because of my race, I go out of my way to understand anyone who is less advantaged than myself. I think many uneducated people are that way because of lack of opportunity and financial backing. I am very compassionate to the poor; I feel for their plight and I am sympathetic to their circumstances. That is why politically and socially I am a social democrat and would pay more taxes if it will help the disadvantaged. The prejudice I have experienced in Canada has made me examine racism. I will not treat another person the way I have been treated. I remain hypersensitive to how I think of others and will continue to grow in this regard. The journey never ends.

Conclusion

The process of re-reading my journals and files and doing the research needed to write my memoir has been a learning experience for me. I had many questions. One was: why did I think so differently about race and slavery than my fellow African Americans? Or: what do I think of my Black ancestors from my African past? I would then explore what the answers to those questions mean to me. An African friend said to me once, "I do not understand you Trinidadians, you never refer to yourselves as African. You always say you are "mixed" and refer to some white ancestry, such as Scottish, English, Irish, French or Spanish, although you are clearly part African."

Another question that a Black American from the south asked me in 1973 was, "How could you fall in love with a white guy?" At the time, I was dating the man I would marry, a white, fifth-generation Canadian of Scottish ancestry. The African American explained that he was a supervisor in a plant in upstate New York. Most of his coworkers were white and male, and he thought he had a pretty good working relationship with them; in fact one of them had become a close friend. But even though this close friend was white, he knew that he could never date his friend's sister. I asked why, and he related a true story, told to him by his grandmother, of a lynching in their hometown in the South. I realize that I do not feel this anger towards whites; my history and experiences were very different from this African American supervisor.

Since race is a dominant theme in my memoir you can imagine my emotional anger, sadness, outrage and helplessness when I turned on my television and witnessed the murder of George Floyd by a Minneapolis police officer on May 25th, 2020. Of course, protests for the murder of George Floyd began in the United States the next day. Protests all over the world followed. There were solidarity marches to end racism and police brutality everywhere. Protests took place in over sixty countries and on every continent except Antarctica. In Canada, protests took place in all ten provinces and all three territories. I went to our local protest march. I had a strong emotional reaction when I saw the protestors. They were about two-thirds white, and about one-third Black or people of color.

As I prepare this memoir for publication, it was with some relief that the jury in Minneapolis found George Floyd's murderer guilty on all three counts. Both President Joe Biden and Vice President Kamala Harris's responses to the verdict gave me optimism that social justice and systemic racism will be addressed. Vice President Kamela Harris said:

"A measure of justice isn't the same as equal justice. This verdict brings us a step closer. And the fact is, we still have work to do."

Change can sometimes take a long time. Often it first needs to uproot deeply entrenched ways that society has done things. Protests against police brutality have happened before, but today they feel different. I believe it is different. I am very hopeful that George Floyd will not have died in vain. I believe his death will make us examine policing all over the world, but will it go further? Many liberal and socially democratic policy makers have said that social justice and ending systemic racism is a priority, but will this affect change in workplaces and in society as a whole? United States and Canada are both still predominantly white societies. In another generation, we are told, that in the U.S., non-whites will be in the majority. In Canada, of course, we need to address the deep systemic racism against indigenous peoples as well.

I do not think this type of change will be immediate. White privilege prevents white people from seeing racism, even though it is occurring around then daily. White parents don't have to worry every time their sons leave their home late at night. They don't have to be concerned with what their sons are wearing when they leave their home: "Please don't wear your hoodie tonight."

There are positive signs, however, that pop up every day. I just heard on the news today that a bookstore that sells publications by Blacks, is sold out of and back-ordered for three titles: *How To Be An Antiracist*, *White Fragility*, and, *The New Jim Crow*. These titles suggest that white readers want to understand the issues for BIPOC (Black, Indigenous, and People of Color). Knowledge is power, a saying that has guided my beliefs in the past; perhaps a greater awareness of racism can help others change the systemic racism inherent in society today.

Here is another true story that was shared with me by a friend. She is the daughter of an Ontario policeman who was eventually promoted to sergeant. She related incidents that she remembers from the early seventies. At that time his police department wanted to integrate the police force with more Black policemen. Six Black policemen were hired. Her father was not pleased. His rants included his thoughts that there was no place in policing for these recent hires, and what was the police force coming to? He regularly had get-togethers with his similarly-minded white colleagues. They would joke about how they harassed these Black cops in the locker room. This harassment eventually was too much for the Black policemen to take and, one by one, they left. She distinctly remembers the day her dad came home and said, "We finally got the last "jungle monkey" off the force." Her father is now retired, and my friend is estranged from him, but the story speaks to how far we have yet to come before racist attitudes can be addressed.

This story is important for another reason: my friend felt comfortable telling it to me.

We had never discussed race before. She was one of my friends who took part in a Black Lives Matter march. Her feeling comfortable enough to tell me this story of racism is also a step in the right direction.

I have shared the protests, the discussions, the stories, but I have not discussed the silence. There is a lot of silence. For example, I posted a chart of examples of microaggressions to my Facebook profile. I got six likes. My popular posts often receive eight times more. Most of my friends are white. My Facebook account is no different. I think the silence that my friends showed to this post is significant. I think that although we are seeing outrage to police brutality and we agree that Black lives do matter, it will take a lot longer for BIPOC to have a seat at the table. The silence I hear comes from the many people who still think systemic racism doesn't exist. In order to implement change, BIPOC need to be in positions of power. They will not begin to be put into those positions until the people currently in power acknowledge systemic racism and try to understand it.

In the United States where the Black Lives Matter movement originated, we still see tremendous opposition to this movement, and only moderate acknowledgement of its aims by lawmakers. The killings of Blacks at the hands of white policemen fit the narrative of critical race theory, wherein Blacks are seen as socially deviant and violent. There needs to be more contact and mixing of whites and BIPOC in work places and in their neighbourhoods. In large cities, this mixing is happening. But what about the smaller cities, like Ashford, the one where Cornerstone hospital is located? It will take a generation for change to happen.

I need to say that diversity is different from inclusion. Diversity is the "what" and inclusion is the "how." Diversity deals with the demographics of your organization. Does your organization have people of color, of different races, a balance of females, and individuals of different sexual orientation? You can do a head count and use this criterion to prove that your organization is diverse. The "how" – inclusiveness - deals with the culture of the organization. Are all ideas heard and accepted? Can everyone contribute? How is everyone treated? Do you feel respected? Only if you can answer yes to these questions is your organization on its way to becoming an inclusive organization.

Diversity and inclusiveness are processes, not end states.

The acceptance of Blacks by whites as equals is a great challenge, but is not unsurmountable. The start will be to broadly educate people about diversity and inclusiveness; to help people understand that microaggressions are unacceptable and need to be addressed; they need to be seen as covert problems in the workplace and that moral consciousness needs to be applied to all people, Blacks and whites, equally. On a positive note, our present awareness is a start in the right direction. I cannot see us going backwards again. Just start with small steps; we will continue with small steps.

My research for this memoir took me to the economic reasons for slavery. In the Caribbean and North America, these have been the main reasons for subjugation of Blacks and people of color, as they have been all over the world. Canada was no exception, with its two-hundred year history of slavery. The reality of the reasons for slavery leaves me with less optimism for change, but I do believe: it needs to happen, and it will happen.

I have wanted to share my journey in a memoir for many years but I am glad I waited until now. My perspectives and views have matured and changed over time. I can see the bigger picture. I have greater self-awareness of the subjugation of people of color all over the world and in Canada where I call home. Canadians have always had a scapegoat. It began with the indigenous population, and continued with the Irish, the Chinese, Japanese, Italians, and Eastern Europeans, and now people of color. This includes all BIPOC: Indigenous peoples, East Indians, Asians, Africans and Blacks from all over the world, including the Caribbean. BIPOC have experienced prejudice for many decades. Critical race theory says these reasons are economic, political and social. Historically, BIPOC have been stereotyped as inferior beings, lacking in intelligence, lazy and untrustworthy. Canada, like the United States, has been a predominantly white society. Blacks are in the minority and have experienced prejudice in accessibility to education, housing, bank loans and employment for generations. They have been racially profiled by the police, and the law persecutes Blacks more severely when they are sentenced. The 2016 census data shows that Black Canadians face a greater economic challenge than white Canadians, regardless of how long they have lived in Canada. This is, unfortunately, a 21st century reality.

I think that there is still a lack of understanding in Canada that immigrants are necessary to maintain a strong economy. Canada needs immigrants. We have a low birth rate and rely on immigration to maintain our labour force. Outside of the refugee system, the Canadian immigration point system cherry-picks the best immigrants world-wide. The "brain drain" experienced by other countries is Canada's gain. Canada's point system criteria include: financial stability and education level. Immigrants who apply to come to Canada are not the poorest and most disadvantaged, but really the more educated and with enough wealth to support their immigration.

Canada also accepts immigrants on humanitarian and compassionate grounds as refugees. I think that many Canadians view most immigrants as having been accepted as refugees; they see these new arrivals as taking their jobs and in some ways aspiring to a better life, one that does not rightfully belong to them. This resentment can best be expressed in the job environment: Blacks and people of color are usually the last hired, first fired. They have fewer educational opportunities. Immigrants suffer challenges to have the acceptance of their foreign qualifications recognized as equivalent. Many immigrants turn to small business ownership. This is an avenue where they can become financially secure but again, they face setbacks when they apply for loans from the established banks to start their businesses. And these are just a few of the many roadblocks immigrants face.

Many economic immigrants see themselves in what can be described as an "asserted identity" (middle class, educated, articulate); they are equal to Canadians. Instead, they have an "assigned identity" (poor, uneducated, disadvantaged) given to them by Canadians.

So how will things change? When will things change? Who will make the changes? I do not see any changes happening quickly, and the changes that are made will be slower than many Blacks and people of color have a right to expect. Hopefully law enforcement is where we will see the first changes. Social media has helped here; there is usually someone who will videotape incidents so that the public can see what actually occurred, instead of the self-serving version of events that we have become used to in the past. In Canada the mayor of Toronto has tabled a motion which will be heard by council that calls for "alternate models of community safety response." The motion calls for the creation of a non-police-led response to calls that do not involve weapons or violence in order to deal with calls that involve individuals experiencing a mental health crisis.

Changes must continue to deal with overt racism, the "in your face" racism. Our hate laws, and Canada's Charter of Rights and Freedoms provide some protection against overt racism. Hopefully greater cultural awareness and awareness of the need for inclusivity will add to the impetus for change. But what do we do about covert racism? What about the microaggressions that occur in workplaces; the racism that begins at the stage of the hiring process? Because this form of prejudice is covert, changes will likely be much slower.

Can my experiences in the two jobs I have discussed in my memoir be repeated today? I still have friends at Ashford hospital where my worst experiences occurred, and they tell me that it isn't much more diverse. The only people of color hired since I left are two Black nurses. It has been nine years!. Because of the lack of diversity, similar behaviours and racism could be repeated. Critical race theory would say that racialized attitudes and beliefs are part of the Canadian psyche, that racist thinking is embedded in our political and social systems, in our laws, and in the way the legal system operates. This is a primary reason why change in systemic racism will take a longer time. As a start to change our legal system, critical race theory is now being taught at the University of Toronto law school and many other universities. This is a good start, but this isn't a tomorrow change.

I have defined my two hospital experiences as microaggressions. Since the 1990's there has been a movement towards political correctness. Partly as a result of this cultural shift, racism has become more covert, more subtle. Current research investigating discrimination within the workplace has revealed the disturbing fact that racial microaggressions are frequent, pervasive, and cause significant harm to both individuals and organizations.

Because microaggressions are subtle, perpetrators are able to deny them and give other explanations for the subordinate's behaviour, such as poor performance or not following the policies and procedures of the organization. It takes more than recognition by the receiver of the microaggressions to prove their case. For change to happen in the workplace, it has to begin with acknowledgement at the top of the organization, followed by extensive training before microaggressions in the workplace can be addressed. Corporations, including hospitals, will only change, however, if there is a financial advantage to do so. Diversity programs have been promoted in the past as having a financial advantage. I'm not sure that there are sufficient statistics to really prove this. Perhaps this is an area for future investigation?

I do think change in our racial attitudes will occur, and is happening now, but I think it will take time - perhaps even a generation or more for us to see significant change. Small steps. Deciding to write my memoir was one small step for me, and it has fundamentally changed me. I have a new understanding of myself and my identity. To paraphrase an observation made by others: it is not enough to 'not be a racist." At this time, when social justice and racial prejudice are pressing problems that need to be addressed, it is more important to be "anti-racist." I have heard the following response often to my discussions on race: "I am not a racist." White friends and colleagues believe that whenever I now talk about race, they have to defend themselves. What I think Black people want from their white friends now is the realization that the discussion is not about them; it is much bigger than one person. What Blacks want whites to do is to listen and ask if there is something more that they can do to help? Anything however small will have an additive effect. What Black people want is understanding; for others to self-examine their actions and beliefs and see if there is anything that they can do differently to support change.

I hope that readers have enjoyed reading about the life experiences of this Black woman from Trinidad who immigrated to Canada and made a life for herself here. If narrating my life experiences has enabled me to understand myself better, perhaps it will enable you to understand yourself better also.

... the end ...

Appendix A

A History of Race Relations in Trinidad

I have researched Trinidad's history from the 1800's to present. I have also traced my Trinidad ancestors who have formed my consciousness and beliefs since childhood. Let's start with some major differences in Trinidad's history that are significant not only for differentiating it from the U.S. but also from other islands in the Caribbean.

Trinidad was governed by Spain but run by the French planters. Trinidad was never a French colony. French planters came to Trinidad mainly from the French islands of Martinique and Guadeloupe after the French Revolution.

The French planters who came to Trinidad had to be Roman Catholics and they had to take an oath of allegiance to Spain. They also had to agree to abide by Spanish laws. The white French planters were granted land. Many free Africans and free people of color also came to Trinidad from the French islands. They received land grants, but only half of what a white person received. But this was still sufficient for some of them to set up smaller sugar plantations in Trinidad, and yes, even to own slaves themselves.

In 1797 the much more powerful British army and navy captured Trinidad without a shot being fired, and Trinidad became a British colony.

Census of Trinidad, 1797

Whites	2,086	12%
Free coloreds/mixed	4,466	25%
Indians	1,082	6%
African (Blacks)	10,009	57%

As the above census numbers show, Trinidad's Black/African population always vastly outnumbered whites. Even after emancipation in 1838 and the introduction of East Indian indentured labourers, the population was still majority African or Black, with colored (i.e. mixed-race) coming next. At this time free, colored/mixed race were African mixed with Spanish, French or English. The white population (from Spain, France and England), were always in the minority.

In 1793, while still a Spanish colony, the governor of Trinidad, Don Jose Maria Chacon, introduced a "Cedula." As some historians have commented, the Cedula was a set of liberal and enlightened regulations concerning the treatment of slaves. The primary difference was that they were to be treated as persons, not as property. Eric Williams, one of Trinidad's foremost thinkers and its first Prime Minister after being granted independence, has written extensively on social and political issues. The following points illustrate how the Cedula regulations were put into practice.

- Slaves were instructed in Catholicism. They couldn't work on holy days, and they had their own priest to say Mass and administer Holy Communion.
- They had adequate clothing and food.

- Their work day was regulated and they were given two hours a day to labour on their own account. Slaves could only work between the ages of 17-65. Women did work appropriate to females.
- On Holy days after mass they had free time for the rest of the day.
- They had to be given adequate beds, blankets and no more than 2 slaves in a room. Each plantation had an infirmary. The plantation owner had to pay for funerals of its slaves.
- If a slave couldn't work, his owner had to take care of his children.
- Masters were to encourage matrimony.
- Punishment could not exceed 25 lashes, which could not result in blood.
- More serious offences were to be reported to the justice.
- If masters and stewards didn't follow this Cedula, they were fined $50, $100 and $200 for the first, second and third offenses respectively.

Eric Williams, *The History of the People of Trinidad and Tobago,* 1962

As you can see, in Trinidad, the practice of slavery was quite different from the practice of slavery in other colonies. Food and clothing were relatively generous and the punishment of slaves was less inhumane. Children born to slaves could eat and play with the children of their masters. This discussion does not negate the brutality of slavery and the slave trade by the Spanish and French. It also acknowledges that rape of slaves did occur in spite of the Cedula but the consensus of historians is that slaves in Trinidad were treated better than slaves in the United States and other islands. I am also not negating that the main reason for slavery was economic and profit driven.

> "The Frenchman and Spaniard, lacking, then and now, the cruder aspects of racial prejudice which, then and now, distinguishes the Anglo-Saxon in many instances, married his concubine….. But concubine or wife, intercourse with slave women produced an increasingly large colored or mulatto element in all the islands." - Eric Williams, *The Negro in the Caribbean*, 1971.

The French planters were bound by the laws of Spanish rule until 1797. After 1797, although formally under British rule, planters and the British governors of Trinidad nonetheless retained the practices established under Spanish rule. Thus, in practice, British governance in Trinidad was more humane towards its slaves than most other British colonies.

Another significant factor here was the growth and emergence of the colored population as the free and educated middle class of Trinidad. Many colored in Trinidad were born free or achieved their freedom through servitude. Education in Trinidad was supported by British regulatory ordinance, and the children of the free coloreds were encouraged to attend school. Increasingly, then, in 19th century Trinidad, colored people found themselves occupying jobs that included teachers, journalists, printers, pharmacists, doctors, solicitors, barristers and civil servants.

All slaves in Trinidad – as well as in all other British colonies - were emancipated in 1838. Emancipation created a large, free, working class in Trinidad. It would take the United States another quarter century to achieve emancipation, and, some might say, another century before Blacks could begin to achieve the same middle-class status as they did in Trinidad.

For most free, colored, middle class in Trinidad, one of the most important qualities to aspire to was the acquisition of culture and intellectual status: being well-read, having the ability to speak and write "good" English, and NOT having an occupation that required manual labour. For many colored people in Trinidad, these qualities were more significant and more important than wealth.

This was the class I was born into and can trace as far back as three generations to the mid 1800's. There were three classes and four main races in Trinidad in the 19th century: the whites at the top, occupying most of the high administrative positions and owning the banks; the coloreds/mixed population second, occupying the middle class and working in the civil service or in professional occupations; and the Blacks and East Indians as two separate races and cultures occupying the third, or working class. All races and classes evolved significantly as the 20th century approached. The white elite could easily ignore the Black and East Indian masses, for they encountered them only in stereotyped class relationships. It was less possible to overlook the existence of the growing Black and colored middle class. Educated Black and colored men and women had a claim, through their command of British and European culture and their respectability, to consideration as equals.

> "They represented a greater threat to continued white control of the society, even though their numbers were relatively few; they held the key to the political and social future of Trinidad." - Eric Williams, *The History of the People of Trinidad and Tobago,* 1962

Even before emancipation, the middle-class coloreds as well as whites sent their children to the Sorbonne, or to Madrid and Oxford, where they became doctors and lawyers. The mixed or colored population was concentrated in the larger cities, while in the smaller villages and rural areas Blacks and Indians predominated.

Trinidad's culture and race relations were significantly impacted by the recruitment of indentured labourers from India. The end of slavery in 1838 created a labour crisis in Trinidad. The now-free Black population was not interested in working on the plantations anymore and wouldn't sign contracts to work there, because even if they were paid, slave-like working conditions still existed and the pay wasn't enough to make a living. Between1845 and 1917 Trinidad turned to India for indentured labourers. Ninety percent came from the Calcutta region of India. In that region of India, the majority of Indians were poor and hungry. The climate in the region was also similar to Trinidad, and they were used to back-breaking agricultural work. Although their indentureship contracts allowed them to be repatriated back to India after ten years, only a small percentage chose to return.

Between 1845 and 1917, the colonial government brought over 143,939 indentured labourers to work on the island's sugar plantations. By the 1900's about half of the Indian population in Trinidad were born there. In 1871 they were 25% of the Trinidad population; by 1900 this had increased to 33%. One significant reason for this increase was the practice of granting crown land to Indians who had completed their contracts in lieu of their passage back to India. It is important to note here that free Blacks had to purchase crown lands. This limited their development as landowners. As a result of this granting of crown lands, 26 village settlements were established on the crown land granted to Indians. As Indians made money from their plantations it enabled them to buy more crown land - over 56,000 acres by 1900. Indians were the main producers of food in Trinidad and reduced the island's dependence on imported foods from other islands. Up to about 1900, the Indians did not mix with the Black population but stayed in their own villages. They were part of the peasantry. Although there was a shortage of Indian women, Indian men tended not to mix with African or creole women.

Catholicism and, to lesser extent the Anglican religion, have been the predominant religious faiths followed by non-East Indians in Trinidad. Christian missionaries saw the East Indians as heathens and their Hindu and Muslim religions as alien. For their part, Black or white Trinidadians didn't try to understand or integrate the Indian community. But by 1900, Indians had developed a fair degree of economic independence; their population numbers and their economic independence made them a group to be reckoned with. After the 1900's East Indians began to form their own middle class and established themselves as druggists, teachers, clerks and entrepreneurs.

In addition to Indian indentured workers, between 1853 and 1866, twenty-five hundred indentured immigrants from South China came to Trinidad to work on the plantations. They left the plantations as soon as they could, because they couldn't take the backbreaking work on the sugar estates. They eventually became gardeners, vendors, butchers and shopkeepers. As an example, perhaps, of how well the Chinese immigrants to Trinidad assimilated, after Trinidad gained independence in 1962, Soloman Hochoy, the son of a Chinese indentured labourer, became Trinidad's first Governor General.

Starting in 1890, Syrian and Lebanese immigrants began to come to Trinidad. They were escaping poverty and oppression in their homelands. They started as peddlers, going from place to place, selling cloth and other goods.

Before the colonial government settled on East Indian indentured workers, they experimented in the 1840's with bringing in Portuguese indentured labourers, primarily from the Maderia area. But the British colonial government did not see the Portuguese labourers as an answer to the labour needs in Trinidad. The Portuguese labourers, after their contracts expired, primarily became gardeners and small shopkeepers.

In the 1800's many Venezuelans began to come to Trinidad. Because they spoke Spanish and were Catholic, they were able to assimilate very well. Many Venezuelans have continued to immigrate to Trinidad and have integrated into Trinidadian society. The recent political and social upheavals in Venezuela have resulted in a surge in Venezuelan refugees into Trinidad and, unfortunately, they have not been well-received.

The hierarchy of white dominance, politically, economically and socially, continued well into the twentieth century. The two largest groups, the Africans and Indians were competitively jostling for status during this time. There was not a lot of trust between these two races as a result.

One advantage the Indians had over the Africans was their social coherence, and the preservation of their religion and culture. By contrast, the Africans came from many different tribes, languages and religions. As a result they were not as socially cohesive.

Under Spanish rule, the emphasis had been placed on the conversion of slaves to Christianity, especially Catholicism. This was not the case with the East Indian population. They resisted joining this foreign religion and, as a result, were left alone to follow their own religions, Hinduism and the Muslim faith.

Although there has been mistrust between the Africans and the Indians, the 20th century has also seen mixing and intermarriage that was almost non-existent a century before. This has resulted in a new racial group of people called "Dougla." In spite of the increased level of intermarriage, the competition between these two groups has remained and has been taken to a political level. The two major political parties in Trinidad, the People's National Movement (PNM) and the United National Congress (UNC) are still based mainly on race: African and Indian respectively, although this may begin to change in the twenty-first century.

Trinidadians of mixed European and African ancestry (colored/mixed) have tended to support the PNM party versus the UNC party. As a result, the African-based party maintained power for many years. Another reason for this dominance of power was education. Indians did not have the same access to education as the mixed population of Trinidad and the upwardly mobile Africans. While the British colonial government in Trinidad supported and encouraged formal education for the colored and Black populations, they suppressed support for education for Indians. As a result many coveted civil service jobs were held by mixed Trinidadians and Africans.

Indians began to succeed in different ways, however. They became small business owners and today are a strong economic force in Trinidad. They have surpassed Africans and the mixed population in terms of their economic success. In 2019 Indians (35.4%) now equal the African (34.2%) population of Trinidad, and own and operate a relatively larger share of small and large businesses in prepared foods, transportation, and the production of goods and services.

Today Indians have caught up in education. The oil revenue contributed to increases in education up to the secondary level all over Trinidad. Indians who were mainly in rural areas of Trinidad have moved into Port of Spain and can be found in all towns and cities in Trinidad.

The Chinese and Lebanese/Syrian groups have also remained in commercial activities.

The Lebanese and Syrians are mainly in Port of Spain and North Trinidad while the Chinese communities are still to be found in small and large communities throughout the island. Chinese have mixed with both Africans and Indians. Although the Lebanese and Syrians are seen as one group in Trinidad, they actually are two distinct groups: Syrians are Arabs or Arameans while the Lebanese are Phoenicians. The Lebanese and Syrians who have intermarried because of the relatively small numbers in each group, see themselves as one group now and they self-identify as "white" Trinidadians, although they are not "white" and certainly not Caucasian.

The breakdown by race in Trinidad in 1963 was as follows:

African 358,558 43%
East Indian 301,964 36%
Mixed 134,749 17%
White 15,718 2%
Chinese 8,361 1%
Lebanese/Syrian 6,714 1%

By 2011 this had changed to:
Total Population 1,215,527
East Indian 35.4%
African 34.2%
Mixed 15.3%
African/East Indian 7.7%
Other 1.3%
Unspecified 6.2%

The 2019 breakdown is almost identical, the total population has increased to 1,394,973

In the late-1960's and early-1970's Trinidad saw the same rise in Black consciousness that was occurring in the United States and other countries. One significant event even had a Canadian connection. The 1969 riots at Sir George Williams University in Montreal, Canada are described in the body of my memoir. In 1970, the governor general of Canada, Roland Michener, was visiting Trinidad and was scheduled to give a speech at the University of the West Indies at the St. Augustine campus. His speech was blocked by protests in reaction to the treatment of the Black West Indian university students by Canadians and the administration at Sir George Williams.

The Black power movement led to a major uprising in Trinidad in 1970. This was to instigate social change in Trinidad. This was also the time that Black students and other Trinidadians marched through the streets of Port of Spain in protests against the discrimination in institutions like the banks who only hired white or mixed Trinidadian of lighter shades (shadeism was institutionalized at this time). The Blacks were protesting against the economic control by a handful of white families which is a travesty when you consider that 95% of the population is non-white and government positions are occupied by Black or mixed race/colored men in positions of power. Eric Williams, the prime minister and head of the governing PNM party, introduced a variety of policies to appease the protesters.

In the 21st century, Trinidad projects itself as a mosaic of races that live together in harmony. The mosaic is true because of intermarriage; many Trinidadians have four or more mixtures. Although on the surface this may be true, when I visit Trinidad today, after fifty years in Canada, I think the color, race and the ethnic divides between them are still alive and well.

I did an informal survey among my Trinidad friends and family of how the colored/mixed population in Trinidad identify themselves racially. A popular term is "red." Yes, they describe most shades of mixtures as red! A lighter skinned "red" Trinidadian with straighter hair may be referred to as white. A single family may have all shades from light skinned to darker brown; the lighter skinned sibling with straighter hair can be called white if mixing with similar friends, but when they are with the browner siblings in the family they cannot. For this reason I question how much Trinidad has changed from when I left in 1969. Back then, I had a cousin who could go to our country club that was whites-only at that time, while her brother couldn't because of his brown skin.

I know there is a much stronger Black identity in Trinidad now, and that many who would have called themselves mixed or colored have discarded that distinction and refer to themselves as Black West Indians, This is especially the case if they have lived abroad. In the UK, USA and Canada there is only one distinction, and that is Black.

Doing your "genetic ancestry" is popular today. I have done mine, as have many members of my extended family. As could be expected, my family's mixtures are between 25-50% African, in addition to a variety of French, Spanish, English, Scottish, Irish and Amerindian mixtures. My brother married an East Indian woman, so his children are fifty percent East Indian in addition to African and European genes. This is significant for my story because it provides some context for how I have been raised and for the choices I have made as a child and an adult.

Appendix B

Examples of Microaggressions

Theme	Microaggression	Message
Not being Canadian	"Where are you from? ….. But where are you really from?"	You are not Canadian. You don't belong here.
Challenge to intelligence and family background	"You have a university degree; your parents must be very proud."	You must be the first in your family to have gotten a degree. Your ancestors are uneducated.
Color blindness	"When I look at you I don't see your color. I don't see a Black or brown person; I see you just like me."	Although put forward as a compliment, it denies an important aspect of your identity.

Criminality (Blacks commit more crime)	More likely to be checked at borders; assumption of guilt after a crime is committed; assumption of dishonesty.	I do not trust you. Blacks are dishonest and they steal.
Denial of racism	"I'm not a racist, I have several Black friends."	My behavior doesn't demonstrate racism and I am not a racist because I have Black friends.
Unconscious bias; wanting cultural conformity to the dominant white group	"I don't like the way you speak; you are too animated, you speak with your hands, you are too friendly."	Change your behavior to be more like mine; conform to my image.

Appendix C

Glossary

The literature is now filled with many words and terms to describe different aspects of racism and the treatment of people of color in today's society. They include:

BIPOC - is an inclusive acronym for <u>B</u>lack, <u>I</u>ndigenous, and <u>P</u>eople <u>Of</u> <u>C</u>olor.

Critical Race Theory (CRT) - is a theoretical framework in the social sciences that examines society and culture as they relate to categorizations of race, law and power. CRT holds the view that law and legal institution are inherently racist and that race itself, instead of being biologically grounded and natural, is a socially constructed concept that is used by white people to further their economic and political interests at the expense of people of color.

Driving While Black (DWB) - a sardonic description of the racial profiling of African American drivers. It implies that a motorist may be stopped by a police officer largely because of racial bias rather than any visible violation of traffic law.

False-Consensus Effect – also known as consensus bias, is a cognitive bias that causes people to overestimate the degree to which their beliefs, values, characteristics, and behaviours are shared by others. For example, the false-consensus effect can cause people to assume that others share their political views, even when that isn't the case.

Microaggressions - everyday verbal, nonverbal, and environmental slights, snubs, or insults, whether intentional or unintentional, which communicate hostile, derogatory, or negative messages to target persons based solely upon their marginalized group membership, most often race.

Microinvalidations - a sub-definition of microaggression, microinvalidations are characterized by communications that exclude, negate, or nullify the psychological, thoughts, feelings or experiential reality of a person of color.

Prejudice - preconceived opinion that is not based on reason or actual experience. When someone decides they do not like someone because of their skin color, this is racial prejudice.

Racism - individual and group-level processes and structures that produce racial inequality.

Shadeism – a form of discrimination based on skin color, also known as colorism. It is a form of prejudice or discrimination in which people who are members of the same race treat each other differently based on how white their skin color is.

Systemic Racism - when racist structures or processes are carried out by groups with power, such as governments, businesses or schools they are systemic.

Unconscious bias (or **implicit bias**) - prejudice or unsupported judgments in favor of or against one thing, person, or group as compared to another, in a way that is usually considered unfair. Unconscious biases are social stereotypes about certain groups of people that individuals form outside their own conscious awareness.

White Backlash - the negative reaction of some white people to the advancement of non-whites. It is a possible response to the societal examination of white privilege, or to the perceived actual or hypothetical loss of that racial privilege.

White Fragility - the tendency among members of the dominant white cultural group to have a defensive, wounded, angry, or dismissive response to evidence of racism.

White Privilege - inherent advantages possessed by a white person on the basis of their race in a society characterized by racial inequality and injustice.

Other Definitions (some Trinidadian)

Dougla – a Caribbean Hindustani word that may mean "many", "much" or "a mix". In the West Indies, the word is used to refer to an Afro-Indo mixed race person.

False Pride - an exaggeratedly high or pretentious opinion of oneself.

French Creole – originally, the definition of creole was someone Spanish, French or English born in the Caribbean; now it generally refers to a colored person who has African and French ancestors.

Liming - hanging around, in a public place or a get-together at someone's home with friends; enjoying the scene.

Tantie - a familiar name given to an aunt.

Uppity - historically used in America to describe Black people who were considered to be acting above "their place" Also used by old white southerners to refer to any Black person who looked them in the eye.

Wining - a sexually suggestive dance practiced mainly in Trinidad and Tobago

Acknowledgements

Jan Figurski, my devoted partner and committed editor who has read and reread my memoir every time I have made additions and changes. As a librarian, a writer, a linguist, and professional editor, he can spot a run-on sentence from a mile away. Thank you.

I would also like to thank my dedicated readers, who painstakingly read my memoir and gave me much appreciated feedback and made suggestions for how it could be improved. I cannot thank you enough.

Anton Allahar
Andrew Camman
Dara Flaherty
Diane Huffman
Kathleen Dindoff
Lawrence Watkins
Lynsey Kissane
Marilyn Cecil-Smith
Sophia Jones
Roger Bartlett

A shout out to Hank Nelson-Abbott. I met Hank at Powder Mountain Ski Resort in Utah, where he volunteered as a guide.

I shared some of my negative job experiences with him and he described what I was experiencing as microaggressions. I Googled this word into my phone and when I returned to Canada I researched it. Thank you Hank. For the first time I had a word to describe my experiences and for that I am very grateful. It is this understanding that gave me the courage to explore this construct, review my journals, and write my memoir.

Bibliography

The following materials were referenced in the writing of this memoir.

Books

Al-Solaylee, Kamal. Brown: What Being Brown in the World Today Means (to Everyone). Harper Collins Canada, Toronto, Ontario, 2017.

Brereton, Bridget. Race Relations in Colonial Trinidad 1870-1900. Cambridge University Press, Cambridge, United Kingdom, 1979.

Brereton, Bridget. Social Life in the Caribbean 1838-1938. Heinemann International, Portsmouth, New Hampshire, 1985.

de Verteuil, Anthony. Seven Slaves & Slavery, Trinidad, 1777-1838. A. de Verteuil, Marabella, Trinidad, 1992.

de Verteuil, Anthony. Trinidad's French Legacy. The Litho Press, Port of Spain, Trinidad, 2010.

Diangelo, Robin. White Fragility: Why its so Hard for White People to Talk About Racism. Beacon Press, Boston Massachusetts, 2018.

Esty, Katherine; Griffin, Richard; Hirsch, Marcie Schorr. Workplace Diversity: A Manager's Guide to Solving Problems and turning Diversity into a Competitive Advantage. Adams Publishing, Holbrook, Massachusetts, 1995.

Martin, John D.; Ferris, Frank D. I Can't Stop Crying: It's So Hard When Someone You Love Dies. Key Porter Books, Toronto, Ontario, 1992.

Ottley, Carlton Robert. Slavery Days in Trinidad: A social history of the island from 1797 to 1838. C.R. Ottley, Trinidad, 1974.

Poitier, Sidney. The Measure of a Man. A spiritual autobiography. Harper San Francisco. A division of Harper Collins Publishers, 2000

Pemberton, Rita; [et al]. Historical Dictionary of Trinidad and Tobago. Rowman & Littlefield Publishers, Lanham, Maryland, 2018.

Williams, Eric. History of the People of Trinidad and Tobago. PNM Publishing, Port of Spain, Trinidad, 1962.

Williams, Eric. The Negro in the Caribbean. Eworld Incorporated, 2012.

Wilson, Trevor. Diversity at Work. John Wiley & Sons Canada, Etobicoke, Ontario, 1996

Articles, Podcasts, Papers, and other materials

Allahar, Anton. At Home in the Canadian Diaspora: "Race" and the Dialectics of Identity. In: Wadabagei, Vol. 13, No. 1, 13 September, 2010. Accessed at URL: file:///C:/Users/Jan/AppData/Local/Temp/

Allahar At home in the Caribbean diaspo ra.pdf. August, 2020.

Alexander, Cecily. Diversity in the Workplace: A critique of [an Insurance Company's] diversity program. An independent study paper submitted to the University of Guelph, School of Hotel and Food Administration, Guelph, Ontario, 1996, as part of the author's MBA program.

Cameron, Stephanie. "The Caribbean in your Supermarket". Toronto Star, Feb. 15, 1978.

Cheeks, Maura. How Black Women Describe Navigating Race and Gender in the Workplace. In: Harvard Business Review, March, 2018. Accessed at URL: hbr.org/2018/03/ How Black Women Describe Navigating Race and Gender in the Workplace

Genderman, Dina. Minorities Who "Whiten" Job Resumes Get More Interviews. In: Harvard Business School, Working Knowledge, 17 May, 2017. Accessed at URL: hbswk.hbs.edu/minorities-who-whiten-job-resumes-get-more-interviews. September, 2020.

Harris K. accessed at URL: www.whitehouse.gov/briefing-room/speeches-remarks/2021,.22April,2021

Immigration and Refugee Board of Canada. Trinidad and Tobago: Racial problems faced by persons of Chinese descent, and state protection available against racially-motivated harassment or violence (1999-2002). In: Government of Canada website, 19 March 2003, TTO40968.E. Accessed at URL: https://www.refworld.org/docid/3f7d4e26e.html. August, 2020.

Jamison, Leslie. "On Female Rage". In: The New York Times, August 2, 2020. Podcast accessed at URL: https://www.nytimes.com/2020/08/02/podcasts/the-daily/onfemalerage.html. August, 2020.

Manning, Jennifer. "Moving from Diversity to Inclusion". In: National Diversity Council Newsletter, Fall 2018. Accessed at URL: http://ndcnews.org/2018/02/27/movingfromdiversitytoinclusion/#:~:text=Diversity%20is%20defined%20as%20a,into%20one%20community%20or%20workplace. August, 2020.

McIntosh, Peggy. "White Privilege: Unpacking the Invisible Knapsack". First published in: Peace and Freedom Magazine, July/August, 1989. Accessed at URL: https://psychology.umbc.edu/files/2016/10/White-Privilege_McIntosh-1989.pdf. August, 2020.

Momani, Bessma. "Immigration is a net economic benefit – this is a story Canada should build on". In: The Globe and Mail, Toronto, Ontario, Sept. 14, 2016, and updated May 17, 2018.

Navarro, J. Renee. "Unconscious Bias". Podcast, University of California San Francisco, Office of Diversity and Outreach, Resources. Accessed at URL: https://diversity.ucsf.edu/resources/unconscious-bias. August, 2020.

Nesbitt-Johston Writing Center. "Language of Difference: Writing about Race, Ethnicity, Social Class and Disability". In: Writing Resources, Hamilton College, Clinton, New York, 2015. Accessed online at URL: https://www.hamilton.edu/academics/centers/writing/writing-resources/languageofdifference-writing-about-race-ethnicity-social-class-and-disability. August, 2020.

NPR (National Public Radio). "Why We Have So Many Terms For 'People of Color'. In: Code Switch Newsletter. Accessed at URL: https://www.npr.org/sections/codeswitch/2014/11/07/362273449/why-we-havesomany-terms-for-people-of-color. August, 2020.

Rampton, Martha. "Four Waves of Feminism". In: Pacific Magazine, Fall 2008. Accessed at URL: https://www.pacificu.edu/magazine/four-waves-feminism. August, 2020.

Savoie, Natalie. Anti-racism and privilege in dietetics. In: Dietitians of Canada, News Updates, 2020. Accessed at URL: www.dieiticians.ca/News/2020/anti-racismandprivilege-indietetics. September, 2020.

Slaughter, George; Singh, Mahima. Five charts that show what systemic racism looks like in Canada. On: CTV News, 4 June 2020, and updated: 6 June, 2020. Accessed at URL: https://www.ctvnews.ca/canada/five-charts-that-show-what-systemic-racism-lookslikein-canada-1.4970352. August, 2020.

Soyluv. Let's Talk About Race, Trinidad. In: Creative Commons, Wordpress.2015. Accessed at URL: https://soyluv.wordpress.com/2015/09/15/lets-talk-aboutracetrinidad/amp/. August 2020.

Wikipedia. Afro-Trinidadians and Tobagonians. https://en.m.wikipedia.org/wiki/AfroTrinidadians_and_Tobagonians. Accessed: August 2020.

Wikipedia. Sir George Williams affair. https://en.m.wikipedia.org/wiki/Sir George_Williams_affair. Accessed: September 2020.

Wing [et al]. "Racial Microaggressions in Everyday Life: Implications for Clinical Practice". In: American Psychologist, V.62:4, 2007, pp.271-286.

Photo Credits

The picture of the author's father's cricket team was taken in 1939 and is in the author's possession. Photographer unknown. The photo is also in the possession of the archives of the Oval Stadium in Port of Spain, Trinidad. Used by permission of the Queen's Park Cricket Club.

Paintings pictured in the memoir are by the author and photographed by her.

All the rest of the photographs in the memoir are photographs of family and friends taken by and in the possession of the author. All people pictured have given their consent to have their pictures included in this memoir.

About the Author

Cecily Alexander has had a career as a dietitian for over forty years. In that time she has also been a loving wife, mother to her three precious sons, and now "grand" to three grandchildren. Her career has included academic writing and she has one previous book publication, a book on nutrition and weight loss: *Just Eat Less: Easier said than done*. She has always written and journaled. This memoir is a collection of many journals she has kept over the years. She finds comfort in writing and uses journaling as her way of working through feelings and emotions. She has a master's in business administration specializing in organizational behavior, in addition to her nutrition degree from the University of Guelph, and she has taught at both the University and College levels. She lives in south-western Ontario, Canada.